And Then the King Died

Alastair Woolley

Dynasty Press Ltd.
19 New Road, Brighton,
East Sussex, BN1 1UF

www.dynastypress.co.uk

First published in this version by Dynasty Press Ltd.

ISBN: 978-1-9161317-7-4

Copyright: © Alastair Woolley 2022

Alastair Woolley has asserted his right under the Copyright, Designs and Patents Act 1988 to be identified as the author of this work.

All Rights Reserved: No part of this publication may be reproduced in any form or by any means without the written permission of the publishers.

Edited by Rosie Stevens

Illustrations on pages 2, 6, 8, 11, 27, 29, 41, 57 & 84 by Tio Wahono
All other illustrations and cover image by Sandusara Kalubowila

Cover design by Rupert Dixon
Typeset by Biddles, Blackborough End, Norfolk.

Printed and bound in the United Kingdom.

To my wife Heather and my grandchildren Alex and Gina

CONTENTS

The English royal line with the inclusion of major rulers of Scotland in *italics*.

INTRODUCTION	ix
The ancient greats	
ALFRED the GREAT	1
EDWARD the ELDER	3
ATHELSTAN	4
The Eds with some Viking interlopers	
EDMUND	5
EDRED	7
EDWY	8
EDGAR	9
EDWARD the MARTYR	10
ETHELRED the UNREADY	12
SWEYN, FORKBEARD	14
EDMUND II, IRONSIDE	16
CANUTE	17
HAROLD I, HAREFOOT	19
HARDICANUTE	20
EDWARD the CONFESSOR	22
MACBETH	*23*
HAROLD II, GODWINSON	24
The Normans (none called Norman)	
WILLIAM the CONQUEROR	25
WILLIAM II, RUFUS	27
DUNCAN	*27*

LULACH, MALCOLM III and sons Duncan II, Edmund, Edgar, Alexander I,
David I ... 28
HENRY I, BEAUCLERC ... 29
STEPHEN ... 31

The Plantagenets (named after a plant, broom)
HENRY II ... 32
RICHARD I, LIONHEART ... 33
JOHN, LACKLAND ... 35
HENRY III ... 36
EDWARD I, LONGSHANKS ... 37
ALEXANDER, MARGARET, JOHN BALLIOL and ROBERT ... 38
EDWARD II ... 39
EDWARD III ... 41
RICHARD II ... 42

Lancastrian kings, (a division of Plantagenets with a red rose)
HENRY IV ... 43
HENRY V ... 44
HENRY VI ... 45
JAMES I and JAMES II ... 46

Yorkist kings, (a division with a white rose)
EDWARD IV ... 48
JAMES III ... 49
EDWARD V ... 50
RICHARD III ... 51

The Tudor kings (symbolised by a red and white rose)
HENRY VII ... 53
HENRY VIII ... 54
CATHERINE of ARAGON ... 56
ANNE BOLEYN ... 57
JANE SEYMOUR ... 58
ANNE of CLEEVES ... 59
KATHERINE HOWARD ... 60
KATHERINE PARR ... 61
EDWARD VI ... 62

CONTENTS

LADY JANE GREY	63
MARY I (Bloody Mary)	64
ELIZABETH I	65
MARY QUEEN OF SCOTS	67

The Stuarts, or Scottish (with a Commonwealth interlude)

JAMES I *(Or VI)*	69
CHARLES I	70
OLIVER CROMWELL (Lord Protector)	73
RICHARD CROMWELL (Lord Protector)	74
CHARLES II	75
JAMES II	77

Orange (not literally)

WILLIAM III	79

Back to Stuart

MARY II	79
ANNE	81

Hanoverian

GEORGE I	83
GEORGE II	85
GEORGE III	87
GEORGE IV	88
WILLIAM IV	89
VICTORIA	90

The house of Saxe-Coberg and Gotha

EDWARD VII	92

Windsor

GEORGE V	93
EDWARD VIII	95
GEORGE VI	96

FINAL INFORMATION	97

INTRODUCTION

From Alfred the Great onwards there have been so many books about British royalty and here is another. There has always been a fascination for the lives and times of kings and queens and here we dwell on their unfortunate deaths. Peering at their last moments which were often very far from fitting for their eventful lives. As may well be expected murder, family illness, death in battle and toilet problems feature with some very sad endings.

The book is a collection of stories from each of the lives of the established lineage of the monarchs of England, with additions from Scotland. It tells of the deaths of the major royalty and ignores the less significant regional rulers of parts of ancient Great Britain (although no doubt some of them had peculiar ways of leaving society). All the stories have entertained people for years and anything humorous in the passages following come from the monarchs or their biographers in earlier times and the stories are certainly worth attention.

The King is Dead, Long live the King, quite simply means there are plenty more where he came from. The dynasty continues and leadership skips from father to son, or actually very often jumps a bit across family lines. No problem or perhaps a little upset.

Some heroic fighting was a necessity for early kings often having disputes with neighbours or Danes.

Some kings had epic victories, like those for Henry V in the Hundred Years War.

Some kings had pyrrhic victories as the country was often lacking in cash after the battles or their extravagant lives. Some had lives that were even more related to the true point that comes from the life of King Pyrrhus who fought and won battles against impressive Roman foe. It was the fact that at the end of all his great exploits King Pyrrhus returned to

Epirus to be killed by an old woman who chucked a brick at him (or a tile). What was it all for? can be the comment made at the end of a number of the following life stories and that is the aspect that made a victory truly "pyrrhic". The similarities with the death of King George II are obvious as he was the last British king to lead the troops into battle and he too died from a bang on the head, as he fell off the lavatory. Perhaps a similar death to that of the American king Elvis (without any allegation of drug abuse).

Stomach problems can soon put an end to lengthy disputes and life's struggles. We can easily think of those with dysentery dying on the toilet, as John and Henry V will have suffered.

As with the whole of society, illnesses being so common there were going to be lots of deaths from health issues. In Scotland Robert I died of leprosy and in England Mary II died of smallpox.

Henry II died of ill health after battling away in France but must have had a deathbed shock when he was given the list of those he was fighting which included his sons and even his favourite, John was against him. Richard II ended up even more deserted and forgotten when he starved to death in Pontefract.

Famously porphyria, which is a hereditary disease causing a lack of production of a vital enzyme in the body and therefore disrupting red blood cell production, has been transmitted through the family with the first symptoms being apparent in Mary Queen of Scots (who lost her head before the illness could see her off). Her son James I (or James VI in Scotland) had the illness and it most likely killed him. Later it is thought that George III died from this illness and that it caused the symptoms that were described as his madness. He used a lot of foul language when ill. Queen Victoria had children who displayed symptoms as well. The disease causes abdominal pain, skin problems, and disrupts the nervous system and provides mental health issues, all unpleasant to deal with when matters of state require attention.

Just as Alexander the Great died at the dinner table so did Edred die, in his case because he spat the food out after chewing it, and spat out nutrients. And as Alexander the Great was embalmed in honey after his death so perhaps should William the Conqueror have been given a

INTRODUCTION

similarly respectful treatment in France because of his advancement of the Norman State. As it was there was a débâcle over his interment which required a financial bribe for it to continue and the dignity of his funeral was disturbed a bit because his fat body split open and the stench was overwhelming.

The pursuit of the good life caused the downfall of a selection of English royalty. Edgar led the way when it came to death by partying and not long later Ethelred the Unready drank himself to death with the excuse given by some historians that he was worried about how he became king (as if that has to be bad luck or would really have upset him when he was getting drunk). George IV speeded his death by the love of women and cherry brandy, although it is also said that Edward IV accelerated his end by the need for pleasure. The prize for taking it too far goes to Edward III by dying after being robbed by prostitutes and by devoting his last years to their services, and delighting in the low life of the time.

When it comes to bad luck at the end of life Scotland had a couple of unusual stories. James II killed by cannon fire in battle, but his own cannon blowing him up, and Malcolm III killed after the siege of Alnwick Castle. When Malcolm triumphed he leant down from his horse to collect the keys and in doing so he stabbed himself through his eye with his own lance. Stories like that always have an element of disbelief attached to them today and that feeling just creeps over the reader as to whether some person had a hand on the lance at the time. Detective work is not the aim of this book and no extra vision is available on those deaths that could benefit from more information than has been given by the popular history books. As with all history there is usually another version of a story to be had. No further insight is available on the plight of the two children who were murdered in the Tower of London (or any answer as to why Uncle Richard did the deed). No extra evidence in the case of William Rufus whose day hunting was ruined, to the advantage of his brother nearby. Not even a clue as to why King George V got sick of Bognor.

The list is long and for this publication a summary of those in England is made, the stories are all well known and none worth more detailed study here. The characters listed had lives and times that are well worth detailed investigation but this book is not going to add the necessary analysis to be worthy of that consideration.

The early kings, like so many of their subjects, had a tendency to die young. Egbert who is considered to be the ancestor of our royal family lived to be seventy, bucking that trend, but he was very much the exception. Sadly for this book, what the early kings died of was largely a mystery as all too often the historians of the day passed on quickly to recording the activities of the next in line.

Egbert (827 - 839), who was long lived had a son Ethelwulf (839 - 858). He was replaced by three sons Ethelbald (858 - 860), Ethelbert (860 - 866) and the early Ethelred (866 - 871) before his fourth son became the famous King Alfred. The names of these early incumbents are often written as Aethelwulf, Aethelbald, Aethelbert or Aethelred but this book drops the silent A as most citizens were illiterate and would not have known it existed anyway, at the time.

Ethelred I (not to be muddled with the later one that was not ready) fought several battles with the Vikings at Reading, Ashdown and Basing. Ethelred suffered serious injuries during the next major battle at Meretun in Hampshire; he died of his wounds shortly after at Witchampton in Dorset, where he was buried. This made way for the first of our kings to get a special mention and the book will now give slight consideration to the leaders in sequence.

❋ The ancient greats ❋

ALFRED the GREAT
871 to 899

It must be very satisfying to sit in heaven and watch and find that you have been awarded the epithet "Great". After dedicating himself to improving learning and religion for the populace and settling a troubled nation he deserves to be famous.

When his father battled himself into his grave he left two young boys and it was decided that one was a better age to rule (always a good idea). Alfred got the job and soon he had to follow the normal family occupation by fighting. Driving Danes out of the kingdom became a family pastime and Alfred was evidently a good choice for leader. Soon followed peace and relative tranquillity with the opportunity for Alfred to build up a navy. He brought scholars from abroad and arranged the writing of laws. He had visited Rome for some time and soon started arranging the nation for its future.

Alfred has been associated with poor culinary skills and there could well be truth in the story that he was left to attend to some cakes and allowed them to burn. At this time, long before a Great Bake Off competition existed to affect his reputation, Alfred was excused. Overall though Alfred was an achiever despite his health.

There is a story that as a child he prayed that his illness would disappear and that if necessary God would replace it with another (so long as he did not have to suffer leprosy or blindness). His prayers were answered in full, his attacks stopped, but another illness followed. The new symptoms of the second illness seem to have been remarkably similar to the previous ones, and they interrupted his wedding in 868. He remained a cheerful character and a well-tempered leader. Living to the age of 50 was something to be considered a bonus.

Whatever his illness was it got him in the end. Haemorrhoids have been given consideration but Crohn's disease has perhaps a stronger standing for the nomination of Alfred's health curse. Debilitating fits could also have featured along with general digestive disturbances (very unpleasant ones). Edred later had something of the same upsets.

Alfred likely died at Winchester but all did not go well for the burial. The new minster he had planned was not ready for the ceremony so he was first buried at the old one. However the younger clergy at the old minster could not wait for him to be moved to the new as he troubled them at night. His ghost would wander about. Once he was moved to what became Hyde Abbey he seems to have settled.

During the reformation incidentally Hyde Abbey was despoiled and the bones of a number of Saxon kings were shoved into wooden caskets and placed above the chancel in Winchester Cathedral. Because the bones got a bit mixed up there is perhaps little chance of his ghost wandering about today.

Alfred's will, when read, left a good supply of money and, best of all, a valuable sword, and also the instruction for the men to buy out the womenfolk if the occasion demanded it. Statues of him would be under threat today, but he is still known as great.

"You silly king eating all those black cakes will play havoc with your digestion, not to mention the acrylamide giving you cancer."

EDWARD the ELDER

899 to 924 (died 24th July 924)

Naturally the first Edward is not Edward I, he comes later which is very British (quite a bit later).

When Alfred had his last fit the throne passed to his son Edward, who ruled a large chunk of southern England but in conjunction with his sister Ethelfled. She died in Tamworth in 918.

Edward has been considered to be a chip off the old block with similar ideals to his father, although not quite the same ability. He was stern and patient and did well routing Danes, so a good fighter.

It seems he was out riding one day and he spotted a shepherd's daughter called Egwina. Despite her name he was in love and she became a regular court special. She gave birth to Athelstan nine months later. He did have a couple of legitimate sons who were young at the time of his death, they were Edmund and Edred who had to wait to rule. Edward did a bit more breeding that needs a mention because he had two other sons. One called Ethelward who died just days after his father, and one called Edwin. Edwin blotted his copybook and was sent to sea to fend for himself. He had involved himself in a conspiracy and needed to be banished. He was not informed that there was a small hole made in the bottom of the boat and sadly he drowned.

Edward the Elder is considered a good king because the wealth and status of the nation rose during his years.

After leading troops he died because of a short, unknown illness in Farndon on Dee which was a royal estate not far from Chester. It has been recorded that injuries from fighting contributed to this outcome. That was an occupational hazard at the time.

ATHELSTAN
924 to 939

Although a bastard Athelstan gets a good reputation for being sensible and a highly respected member of the royal lineage. So not a bastard to his subjects.

When his father died Athelstan was already 30. He was said to be good looking with flaxen hair, medium height, thin, and of course, rich.

He was also a good warrior and he won the Battle of Brunanburh (wherever that might be). An impressive battle at which it was claimed five kings and seven earls died, but not Athelstan. It was under the rule of Athelstan that the kingdom grew in size to include parts of both Ireland and Scotland as well as the whole of Wales.

During this reign an important character called Dunstan crops up in our history for the first time, but is sent into exile for being a bad influence. This character returns to torment future kings but Athelstan knew how to deal with him. Dunstan was a holy man who became a saint but Athelstan did not require his help.

Again poor Athelstan had regular bouts of illness similar to his grandfather and other family members. One of these sessions killed him at the age of 44. Another death from the likely digestive upsets of the family.

A very much respected king and strangely the name never caught on for future regents to use, unlike his father Edward.

🌸 The EDs 🌸

EDMUND
939 to 946

When Athelstan died one of Edward's other sons came to the throne. Edmund had been raised by his half-brother and had fought alongside him at the famously unknown battleground of Brunanburh. All auspices were indicating that Edmund was going to be a good influence on our nation. He had all the necessary qualities and pedigree to lead and was enjoying life to the full.

Athelstan had banished the famous character called Dunstan but Edmund had second thoughts. The story goes that Edmund was out riding one day and his thoughts went back to the day Athelstan threw out the holy man. Just at that point Edmund's horse bolted and headed for the edge of Cheddar Gorge. Although he had some lovely views Edmund thought it some sort of omen. Just before the edge the horse veered away and Edmund lived to face another death and at the same time he decided to give Dunstan a bit of consideration.

Unfortunately in 946 the king turned up at a banquet in Pucklechurch, in Avon. The event to celebrate was St. Augustine's Day, 20th May and it was a drunken sort of affair with plenty of ale. The king never left it alive. Soon after the main course he was stabbed to death.

At the same party was Leofa whom the king recognised as an undesirable character, a robber, whom he had banished some six years earlier. Edmund approached the bloke to explain to him in a physical way that he was not welcome. Leofa had an alternative point of view. Sadly Leofa picked up a knife and stabbed the king. He was then torn limb from limb by the other guests but Edmund's reign was over. The funeral was a lavish event held at Glastonbury Abbey.

And Then the King Died

"Dreadful, Leofa has killed the king. Poor Edmund would want us to get lots more ale for his funeral."

EDRED
946 to 955

Historians have portrayed this next young king as a good warrior and a worthy king. He did defeat the eponymous Eric Bloodaxe from York but the Saxon troops who helped were a skilled force. Dunstan seems to have had a great influence during this reign.

Poor Edred seems to have had nasty digestive problems throughout his life. He was always a weak child suffering "continual languor" and he grew into a fine weak adult. Never the life and soul of the party, at banquets he upset many guests by chewing food and instead of swallowing the solids he would spit them out. Not table manners to be recommended but as a king he still had invitations. Eating was not his forte but perhaps he drank a lot.

Edred got steadily weaker and did not manage ten years of rule.

He died a bachelor in Frome on 23rd November 955 and was put to bed with a shovel in Winchester Old Cathedral.

EDWY

955 to 959 (sometimes called Eadwig)

When Edred faded away his nephew Edwy was next on the list to be king. He was known as the "All Fair" and indeed he could have been on the list of notable kings. Where the previous monarch had encouraged Dunstan and taken his advice, Edwy did not see eye to eye with the future saint. This was undoubtedly his downfall.

The troubles probably started on the occasion of the coronation day when Dunstan (who considered himself to be next to God) found Edwy in amorous activity with a young lady and not attending to his duties. In fairness to Edwy he did marry her and at seventeen his enthusiasm for her was not unnatural. Elgiva, who became Queen, did not like Dunstan and became a constant enemy.

So the king banished Dunstan from court once more, and sent him away penniless. As many will have expected he returned but with the king's younger brother, Edgar. A short civil war followed which Edgar won.

What happened to Edwy is not properly recorded. Could the reason for this be that clerical historians would have been influenced by Dunstan, a man of the cloth? It may well be that poor young Edwy met his doom in some dark alley so that there was no chance of a comeback fight. This seems likely, history has recorded this death as a definite murder.

"Oh look, a dead king."

EDGAR

959 to 975 (born approximately 943)

So it was that younger brother Edgar received the leadership, with Dunstan.

As for Edgar, he seems to have been a strong enough person, ostentatious and a leader. Dunstan's help ensured a favourable press and he seems to have patronised the church. However there was an immoral side to his character.

There were few troubles recorded in this reign, and that has to be good. This was the king who was flamboyant enough to be rowed over the river Dee by six other regional kings. Another story was that he challenged the king of the Scots to a duel (which the Scottish monarch backed out of). Bearing in mind that Edgar was a tiny little man, that showed guts.

His weakness of flesh was well known, his coronation was held up because he loved the good life (for thirteen years). He killed the husband of his wife Elfrida, (a hunting accident?) who herself was no innocent damsel.

Edgar died suddenly aged 32, but there was a strong suspicion that drink and the good life contributed to his passing. He died in Winchester on 8th July 975 and was buried in Glastonbury Abbey.

He left a son and a daughter from his first marriage, Edward and Edith. Also from his marriage to Elfrida he had a son who died young and another called Ethelred who features later in the tale of royal lineage. Not all his children were legitimate, he seemed to live well. The throne now passed to son Edward.

EDWARD the MARTYR

975 to 978 (born around 962 but unknown)

Another Edward and still not the first (we have to wait longer for the first). From his given regnal name above it is not difficult to determine that this reign is not going to go well.

As described in the previous chapter, Edgar died and left the throne to his elder son Edward. However the queen thought her son Ethelred was ready and more appropriate to take over.

Edward seems to have had a bad temper and therefore it is strange that he should have been made a saint on his death. He was born in about 962 and therefore was quite young in 975 when he took over England. Dunstan was around to help, and his step-mother, Elfrida, was around to hinder.

So on 18th March 978 while out hunting with friends he decided to call round and see how his step-family was getting on at Corfe Castle. It had been a tiring day so he popped in to be given a drink. Sadly the waiter stabbed him in the back and his budding career came to an abrupt halt.

One version of the story has Edward leaving the castle with the knife still in his back and slowly dying, as he fell from his horse it dragged him back to his followers for him to die in their arms.

What was true was that killing a king was going to upset the population. These were violent times, but killing a king who has divine rights was bad news.

The king was buried at Wareham and his tomb became a place of pilgrimage. One story was that Elfrida also made a trip to pay homage at the tomb but her faithful horse would not go close. As a result Elfrida gave up and went to live out her life in a nunnery.

EDWARD the MARTYR

"Well I don't think he was very welcome!"

ETHELRED the UNREADY

978 to 1013 (deposed and died 1016)

Mother had made the arrangements so that Ethelred was now king. He had an independent outlook for the job and was a very young man being born in 968. It has been said that the circumstances of him getting the job were difficult for him and affected his reign. His line (and his wife's) versus the Vikings was the scene for the next few years.

He liked the good life. He slept a lot, liked the women, and drank a lot. But we know he was not all good because he was not well liked.

During the early years he cannot have been ready. Danish troops invaded and even burnt London, which must have been upsetting. The king had a novel solution to the problem, he paid for the raids to stop. The real meaning of "unready" is said to be "redeless" meaning having bad advice.

The bad advice was proven as the pay-offs did not work. Some were huge for the time - £24,000 or £30,000-, yet raids returned. These payments of "Danegeld" as they were known did not stop attacks throughout Ethelred's reign.

Sweyn took control of the country while Ethelred continued his riotous lifestyle. Perhaps the death of his half brother bothered him throughout?

Poor Ethelred died on 23rd April 1016 two years after being deposed, and some thirty eight years after the death of his sibling. Drink and partying accelerated his end.

Interestingly his widow married Sweyn's son Canute and had a second shot at being Queen.

There was nothing very funny to write about his death except to say it was much appreciated.

Scotland

In Scotland it is worth noting that Malcolm II took the throne in March 1005. He did this by killing Kenneth III at Monzievaird. Kenneth had ruled since 997.

Malcolm II was the son of Dubh. He beat the Cumbrians at Carham in around 1016 and increased the size of Scotland to about its present level.

Ethelred in England was king at the start of that millennium with nine more kings in the first century. How much the concept of a job for life was driving them to be king we do not know, but reigns come and go.

The Viking types

SWEYN, FORKBEARD
1013 to 1014

In order to keep the Vikings a little apart the order of dates has been jumbled a bit. Sweyn, whose name seems an ideal one for a hearty drinker, was the man to kick out Ethelred. Unfortunately he was not destined to rule for long. In fact 40 days was his limit. The name gets various spellings as with all early rulers so he should probably be known as Mr. Forkbeard. He was the first Viking ruler of England and son of Harold Bluetooth of radio fame.

He collected plenty of Danegeld which should have set him up to enjoy life in England but just the opposite was his experience. He and his followers may not have been welcomed with open arms by the population. For example his sister, Gunhilda, was beheaded in London after seeing her husband murdered and her son transfixed by four spears.

Sweyn Forkbeard died on the road between Gainsborough and Bury (St. Edmunds) on 3rd February 1014. Gainsborough in Lincolnshire was probably his base but he got round the south of England a bit. His death was a total shock, although he had evidently talked about its potential to his son, Canute. So he achieved the shortest reign – longer than many had hoped.

It is possible that his heart gave out or perhaps some common illness gripped him a bit too hard. His sudden death seems to have been natural, and his body was returned to Denmark. His first son got Denmark and second son England.

There is another version of his death written by John of Worcester and others. It is a version that may have circulated soon after his death and persisted to be recorded much later. This version states that the long dead Saint Edmund hopped out of his grave in order to kill the Viking king on behalf of Anglo Saxons. This he did either by banging him on the head, or stabbing him with a spear, lance or other pointed instrument.

SWEYN, FORKBEARD

So was Sweyn killed by the ghost of St. Edmund the first patron saint of England? Well Canute rebuilt the Abbey at Bury and gave offering for the Saint at his shrine for insurance against a similar event.

"Was the ghost of our English saint defending the crown from the Scandinavian or was his death natural?"

EDMUND II, IRONSIDE

1016 to 1016 for weeks only

Edmund the son of Ethelred the Unready was born in 989 and was therefore now old enough to rule, but Canute was the constant competition. He was also fit enough being described as a burly man, full of vitality and vigour, the nickname Ironside describing his constitution. By November he was dead in Oxford.

There was a strong rumour that the servants of one Edric bumped him off. When Canute heard about this he called the servants to see him. When they visited Canute it was said that they boasted of their actions and Canute gave them a piece of his mind, and they were ushered out of his presence to their immediate execution.

The story continued with the above Edric administering about a third of Canute's kingdom for some time before overstepping the mark and upsetting the king. He supposedly told Canute what he thought about him and also said what a lot of trouble he had in arranging the death of Edmund to help the king.

Far from Canute slapping him on the back and shaking him by the hand he shook him firmly by the neck and threw his lifeless body out of the window into the River Thames.

So perhaps Ironside was terminated by Edric but the man got his due deserves and Canute continued to rule.

It has also been reported that Ironside was stabbed to death while sitting on the toilet over a pit and therefore becoming the first royal toilet death. The death while attending to a bodily function would have provided a good deal of humour in these days, sadly the appeal has waned a bit over the years, particularly as it was a murder as well. In this era the lavatory was particularly funny because nothing else in life could compete for laughs.

A short reign for a promising member of the Saxon line.

CANUTE

(also known as Cnut), 1016 to 1035

Son of Forkbeard next came Canute. He married Ethelred's widow which was a good move (although she was not Ethelred's only wife).

Canute was actually a wise and sensible ruler and he did not drown. The story of him sitting on the beach and commanding the waves to retreat is just nonsense. It seems that history has wrongly included him on the list of mentally inferior kings when actually he did know about the tide. The story is really used today as a way of saying Canute was trying to tell people a king has no divine super ability, as at the time, evidently some did consider him to be so possessed. He developed the rule of a northern area including Iceland, Norway and Denmark and he spread the Christian message. Also his rule boosted the national coffers as paying Danegeld was no longer necessary.

His actual death came as a result of a short illness in Shaftesbury on 12th November 1035. He had ruled for nearly 20 years and was 40 years old.

He was buried in the old cathedral in Winchester which was rebuilt by the Normans and therefore his bones were amongst those scattered many years later by Roundheads in the civil war. They mixed up the bones of several old English kings in caskets at that time in the 17th century.

Canute had left instructions for his son Hardicanute to take over which upset other sons.

Scotland again

In Scotland there was a bit of jostling for their throne. In November 1034 Duncan I (also known as Duncan the Diseased) took over the throne from Malcolm II, who may have died naturally. Duncan was his grandson and was 33 years old. His mother was Bethoc, the daughter of Malcolm, but the leadership was challenged by a rival spur of the family led by the famous Macbeth.

Duncan was indeed killed by Macbeth at Pitgaveny near Elgin in August 1040 thereby giving Shakespeare, or someone very similar, a good story for future use.

HAROLD I, HAREFOOT
1035 to 1040

When Canute died he wanted his son Hardicanute to take over but he was miles away in Norway and in no hurry to come over to England.

One of Ethelred the Unready's children called Alfred had a claim to the throne but he was blinded nastily by a Hardicanute supporter, so nastily in fact that he died from the infected wound.

The illegitimate son of Canute and Ethelred's wife Emma of Normandy grabbed the opportunity. This was Harold who did not take charge for very long.

Harold died of ill health on 17th March 1040 and it seems he was a worried man, very troubled about his legal status. But he had ruled for a short term and was hardly very old, only 24 when he died.

Natural causes seem to have taken him away but he did know that Hardicanute would soon have come to take the job from him. Weeks after his burial Hardicanute arrived and had Harold's body dug up and beheaded, and also then thrown into the Thames. Not terribly pleased that he had kept the throne warm. The bits of his body were fished out of the river and buried at St. Clement Danes in London.

Kings of this era had little regard for other siblings (or the pollution of the Thames).

"Isn't that the head of state?"

HARDICANUTE (or Harthacanute)

1040 to 1042 Son of Canute

Now that Harold had stopped breathing Hardicanute was able to take over and dominate the country. He was extremely unpopular but he did have some supporters and one of these allies was an Earl Godwin who became an advisor. He had supported Hardy even while he was abroad.

Hardicanute set about misgoverning England and as well as being violent he seems to have had a hobby of drinking.

He was drunk when he died because he was having a good time at a friend's wedding, some say he was just toasting the bride. The host was Tovi the Proud and the king suffered an apoplectic fit (a stroke or perhaps an alcoholic induced illness?) probably dying and missing the Best Man's speech. The king was not greatly mourned. He was only 24 so the potential for a costly reign was averted.

Banquets were favourable times to drop dead. Earl Godwin also had a problem at the table. Edward (the next king) had accused the Earl of killing Alfred (the chap blinded in the previous reign) but Earl Godwin naturally protested his innocence. Unfortunately the words he used were not ideal as he said God would strike him down if he had done such a thing. He then proceeded to choke on a piece of bread. This death became legendary at the time.

HARDICANUTE (or Harthacanute)

"He has more than had a few, he has had his last."

EDWARD the CONFESSOR

1042 to 1066 (born 1003 and died 5th January 1066.
His mother was Emma of Normandy)

Still waiting for Edward 1st.

Another of Ethelred's children with Emma was next on the throne (that is another half-brother of Hardicanute). Remembering that one of his brothers had been blinded he sucked up a bit to Earl Godwin at the start so that he was confirmed as king by the Witan*.

Edward was actually a weak character who had luckily kept clear of events by living in Normandy. One story of his reign involved a thief who helped himself to some of the crown jewels. Edward told him to hurry up and how to escape. Edward was a deeply religious man and no doubt cared for his fellow men, certainly not a warrior. He was thought to have remained celibate despite marrying Edith who was Earl Godwin's daughter. He was also most likely an albino.

Edward brought a number of Norman leaders into the country a while before the famous conquest. Earl Godwin also took a fair share of the decision making.

Towards the end of the Confessor's reign another Edward arrived in England. This one was called Edward the Exile because he had lived in Hungary. He was the only surviving representative of the House of Egbert with a true claim to the throne. He lived in England for two days before dying. Perhaps the change of food, or perhaps the weather, he did not last long enough in England to cause any upset, except he did have a son who had a claim to the throne but that was ignored, and that son lived into his sixties.

Edward the Confessor died in the famous year 1066, leaving the title deeds very far from clear. General ill health had weakened him and the news of his project, Westminster Abbey, being completed did not help his recovery from tiredness and weakness. Sometimes he lost speech and then rallied or improved only to fade away just days after the Abbey was completed. He was in his sixties when he died and that was old for a king of his era.

His tomb in the Abbey was a scene of miracles, so they say, and also there is a theory that his body did not decay. It is unlikely that this has been checked recently.

*The Witan was never really a parliament but it was an advisory group that had existed for years to help royalty with decisions.

Scotland

In Scotland Macbeth was slain by the future Malcolm III at Lumphanan near Aberdeen (about 17 years after Macbeth had murdered his father, Duncan I). Mr. Macbeth was the husband of Gruoch the grand-daughter of Kenneth III. Two characters who are little remembered for their patronage of the church.

HAROLD II

(Harold Godwin or Godwinson) 1066 to 1066.
The one who got it in the eye

A very well-known death. But Harold had little claim to the throne, except that his father was the well known Earl that had been active in previous reigns. That made him brother-in-law to the previous king (his sister married Edward the Confessor). The Witan chose Harold to be the next king.

Very soon after being chosen he had to fight off a challenge from his brother Tostig (Godwinson) and Harold Hardrada (who was King of Norway). He won the battle at Stamford Bridge and killed that pair. Then his army had to make the long journey south at speed to Hastings to try and rid the country of William. He failed and ended the era of Anglo-Saxon kings.

The battle started on 14th October with the king's body being identified by armour at the end. He may well have been shot in the eye as the Bayeux tapestry is said to show, but certainly he died a very famous death while fighting.

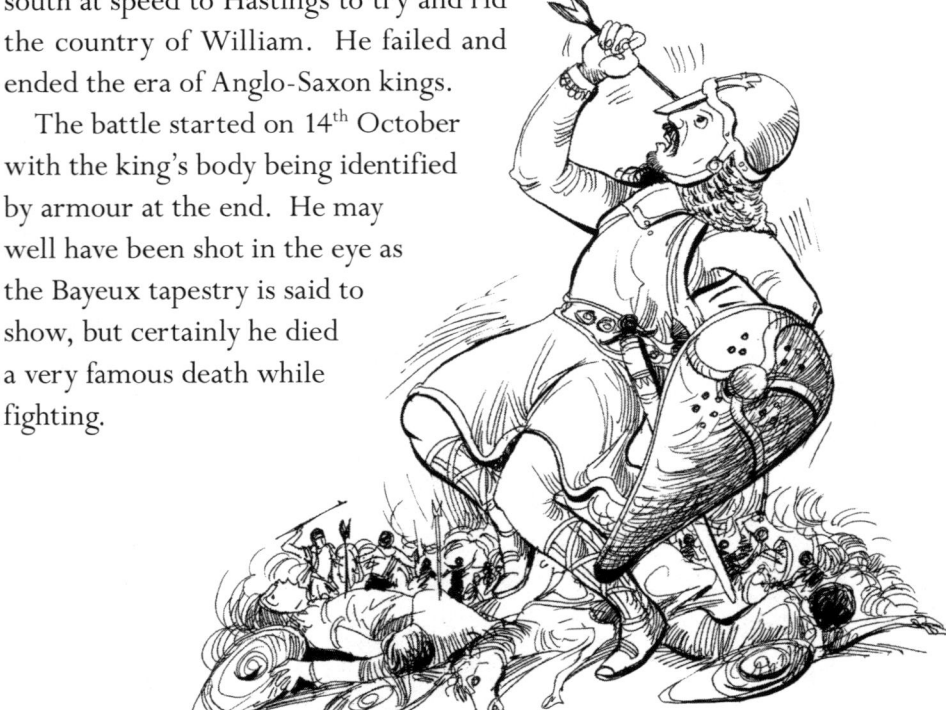

"Look out." "Too late." "Kids will love this story!"

❦ The Normans ❦

WILLIAM the CONQUEROR
1066 to 1087
Born 1027 and died 9th September 1087

Also known as William the Bastard, though few would have dared call him that at the time, the next ruler invaded from Normandy in 1066, providing one of the most famous dates for children to know. Poor Harold had to battle in Yorkshire and make a very quick trip to Hastings. The battle ground at Stamford Bridge was very near York and therefore many miles from Chelsea and many more from Hastings or Senlac Hill (or as we now say Battle, West Sussex). The army would have been tired but fought hard. Harold may have been shot in the eye, although that is uncertain, but he definitely got killed.

William's father was the appropriately named Robert the Devil, who had left the family for a crusade when William was eight and never returned. He was Ethelred's great nephew by marriage.

When William won the battle of Hastings he quickly captured London and was crowned on Christmas Day. He also brought relatives and supporters from Normandy and started building wonderful and sturdy castles. The English systems were being changed fast.

William did not speak English but has to be congratulated for writing the Doomsday book. The actual author involved used mediaeval Latin with many abbreviations to produce a very difficult text that is considered to be the most important English book for the age, despite its lack of legibility.

The King of France upset William when he was ill. Because our William was fat he said William was a long time lying in. So William set off to war again in France, and he loved a good fight. When at the siege of Mantes he sustained internal injuries from an accident he had on his horse, the end was inevitable. A fitting end to a fighter, he made arrangements on his deathbed for the crown of England to be passed on. He bequeathed the Duchy of Normandy to his first son, his second son had already died, but his third son got England while his fourth son got £5,000 along with the remark that all he had to do was wait. He was correct, all young Henry, the number four son, had to do was wait.

William's body was transported to Caen to be buried at St. Stephen's Abbey (built as a dispensation for his marriage). Just as the body was about to be committed to the grave a young Norman knight stopped the proceedings claiming that the grounds of the Abbey were taken from his father and that the bones of the plunderer were not to be associated with his father. A deal was struck at the graveside and the ceremony continued.

He was very fat and his body split open as he was being buried in the normal size grave, so the resulting smell was overpowering and upset the congregation badly.

William had married Matilda of Flanders who was a relative of the English Saxon old ruling clan. Sadly she had died in William's arms in 1083 after dreadful bouts of melancholy. She was buried in another Abbey, Holy Trinity Abbey, which was also built as a dispensation for their marriage. She may not have spent a massive percentage of her married life in his arms but that had given her time to make the Bayeux tapestry.

WILLIAM II, RUFUS

Rufus 1087 to 1100 (born 1057)

William II was the third son of the Conqueror and was known as Rufus because he had red hair. This aspect of his appearance was obviously important in those days. Much hated for his cruelty and reckless extravagance this was a very unpopular leader and some relief may have been felt when he was found dead in the New Forest in 1100. He was slain by an arrow while out hunting, a nasty accident, or perhaps not. William Tirel shot the arrow and nobody really mourned the death. Rufus was buried in Winchester Cathedral without much ceremony. He had never married.

So by coincidence as daddy had dealt with Harold so Mr. Tirel had dealt with son Rufus. Thirteen unlucky years on the throne and his life was all over on a hunting jolly. Tirel left for France quickly in case the murder concept caught on, but Rufus was never well liked and the death was considered to be bad luck as many accidents did happen while hunting.

Scotland.

An update on Scottish problems shows more difficult and dangerous times and the era of Malcolm and sons.

Duncan I also known as Duncan the Diseased reigned from 1034 to 1040 and was

"Never mind leave him there and we join Henry quickly."

Scotland continued...

removed by Macbeth who ruled from 1040 to 1057 until killed by Malcolm III.

Lulach became king for a short spell from 1057 to 1058 (he was a stepson of Macbeth) before Malcolm III killed him as well.

This enabled Malcolm III, the son of Duncan I, to reign from 1058 to 1093 and it was he who supposedly stabbed himself in the eye at Alnwick, once again reminiscent of Harold in England and unlikely an accident. Malcolm had also done a bit of breeding with two wives and his various sons only had to wait.

Brother Donald Bane followed Malcolm III, he was also known as Donald III, and he was soon replaced by Malcolm's son Duncan II. Later poor Donald Bane had his eyes destroyed by another son of Malcolm called Edgar, but Bane had a short reign from November 1093 to May 1094 when son Duncan took over. After Duncan II was killed at Kincardine Donald Bane did return for a while from November 1094 with help from yet another son Edmund. Soon his not being able to see left only Malcolm's sons in charge.

Duncan II was murdered on the orders of half-brother Edmund, who was never actually crowned and eventually became a monk and living in England. This was a good move as he was therefore able to die peacefully.

Son, King Edgar may have been killed but probably actually died peacefully in Edinburgh.

Son, Edward had died young after being wounded at the battle at Alnwick soon after his father, and son Ethelred became an Abbot therefore he died peacefully.

Son, King Alexander I became king in 1107 and died peacefully in Stirling and son, King David I continued the family rule, also with a natural end in 1153.

Malcolm III had left a muddling family period for all, including difficult times for Scottish people.

HENRY I
1100 to 1135 (born 1068)

Also known as Henry Beauclerc.

He was there when his brother died in the New Forest and started his reign immediately. This did lead to conspiracy theories but many actually have always thought that his brother's death was a genuine accident. Henry did arrange better laws for England and therefore his reign has to be an asset. Sadly his two sons died in a ship accident known as the white ship event. The ship sailed from Barfleur in France but hit a rock outside the harbour and they drowned. Nearly all on board perished but alcohol had a lot to do with the accident. Luckily Henry had taken another vessel, but after him there was going to be a dispute about succession as the Normans were getting few in number.

He died as a result of food poisoning on 1st December 1135. The death has amused people ever since as it was recorded as being due to him eating a surfeit of lampreys while in France. The lamprey has dropped out of fashion as a delicacy, for some reason, even in France where there is a history of eating most things that move, but Henry loved them and something transferred the bacteria to his gut that caused his end. The

"You have to love those slippery critters."

idea that one self-respecting and undercooked lamprey did the damage is reasonable, considering the lamprey's own likely feeding habits.

He was buried in Reading in an Abbey that was destroyed by Henry VIII later (as with all other Abbeys) and therefore he is buried somewhere under Reading. Like Richard III he could be under a car park. Or somewhere in amongst the ruins which might well be better presented as a car park*.

He had loads of illegitimate children but who was to come next?

*The potential for him to have spent some of his death under the car park for Reading Gaol is limited but some local residents would appreciate the Abbey complex becoming a car park to improve the town..

STEPHEN

1135 to 1154
(born 1097, died 25th October 1154)

Henry chose his daughter Matilda to rule next but the role actually went to Stephen, a grandson of William I. This caused a bit of a civil dispute. Stephen's mother was a daughter of William the Conqueror, and he had been in Henry's royal court.

A very weak king who had troubles with the neighbours in both Scotland and Wales. Also Matilda did not give up her family claim because she had a son (Henry II, up next). Matilda had married Geoffrey Plantagenet. So Stephen had to battle away his period in charge. His character seems to have been affable, amiable and full of bull.

As with the previous king he died of a stomach illness at a priory in Dover and was buried at Faversham Abbey, but before he died he settled the dispute with Matilda and agreed to her son taking the top job.

❧ The Plantagenets ❧

HENRY II
1154 to 1189

The crown now passed back to the line of Henry I as his daughter, Matilda, had married Geoffrey Plantagenet and had a son Henry II. Henry continued making sensible laws and keeping the finances on course. However one big aspect of his reign kept his name forever notable and that involved the church. He had troubles controlling the actions of the Archbishop of Canterbury, the famous Thomas à Becket. Sadly the king made the regrettable comment, or question "Who will rid me of this turbulent priest?". It was overheard and four of his mates rushed off and murdered Becket thereby answering the question.

Henry was guilt ridden and desperately troubled. Responsibility for the murder of a person close to God was extra upsetting and his wife, Eleanor of Aquitaine, probably did not give much support (she also had affairs). Nor would any of his four sons as they were also prone to adding to his worries.

His sons Geoffrey and Henry were against him and when both of his other sons Richard and John were also causing him problems he grew ill.

Richard was particularly after taking his father's kingdom.

Henry was an intelligent man but he had big family problems. He spoke several languages but English was not one he bothered with. His kingdom included growing areas of France so he did well for England. He wanted his sons to follow him but he ended his life sad and when he developed a fever with a bleeding ulcer, he died.

Eleanor, his wife, actually ruled on with son Richard for a while, as Richard was in the Holy Land, but then she turned to religion and took the veil as so many queens do. It seems she tired of infidelity. She died in her eighties.

RICHARD I, LIONHEART
1189 to 1199

Two of Henry's sons died early. Henry from natural causes and Geoffrey from an unnatural cause because he was jousting and lost. Richard was the second son and he succeeded (Geoffrey was the third son and he was illegitimate anyway and John had to wait). Father had problems with Richard and now it was England's turn to have problems with him.

At 32, said to be handsome and full of courage, Richard had a splendid coronation and soon set about proving that his God was best and that the Middle East needed to change. So he went crusading and showing his "Coeur de Lion" ability as he joined the third such mission. He gathered all the money he could by selling, taxing and borrowing and set off to upset everyone, including his allies. It is strange that history and Robin Hood have recorded him as a good king, valiant and loving of his people. However it is true that when he heard that his brother John had come to England and started being tricky, and possibly making moves to take full power, Richard abandoned the crusade and rushed home. This trip had to be in disguise because of enemies and indeed he was captured in Austria. There is a story of him singing away in his cell and the noise being heard by a trusting, and loyal, troubadour who was passing by at the time. Richard's mother arranged a rescue which cost England dearly (although it was worth it to replace John).

So Richard came back to England and soon had to go and battle the French. He only spent a matter of weeks in England in his whole life. He was killed when besieging a castle at Châlus in southern France, and therefore died a warrior's death. A bolt from a crossbow hit him in the shoulder and a few days later gangrene set in. It was said that a boy shot him and that Richard forgave the youngster on his deathbed. However the forgiveness was forgotten and after Richard died in his mother's arms the child was flayed.

The news of Richard's death upset his pregnant sister badly causing premature birth, and her death as well.

Richard had married Berengaria of Navarre but it has been suggested that the marriage was never consummated. She went to live in a convent and died naturally there.

"Nasty kid!"

JOHN, LACKLAND
1199 to 1216

The favourite son of Henry II but for all others a much despised king (except in King's Lynn and neighbourhood).

Vice rules okay, he took over from his brother bringing new depths of inefficiency, greed and unscrupulousness to the crown. His nephew Arthur also had a claim to the throne as he was the son of Geoffrey who was John's older brother. So John murdered him.

Next John upset the pope over his choice of Archbishop of Canterbury. Following this he upset the English barons who were led by the new archbishop. However the barons forced the king to sign Magna Carta and as a result John set the foundation for our constitution and judicial system. This should have recorded him as a great king but actually John then dedicated his activities to removing Magna Carta.

He also lost the crown jewels in the Wash. This seems careless but it is actually considered it was far more likely that he really spent or gambled them away. They have certainly remained unfound.

He is much loved in the North Norfolk area despite the fact that they killed him. He contracted food poisoning from his visit and died of dysentery. This has been described as him dying of a surfeit of peaches and new cider, but local shellfish could well have been involved.

There was also a theory that one of the monks at Swineshead Abbey (a short distance up the A17) poisoned the king's ale and that the monk drank from the cup first. Although John stayed at the Abbey after losing our jewels it is unlikely that this story described the way he met his end and it was more wishful thinking.

He just died getting weaker from the shits ready to hand on the crown to his young son (except he had lost it). He spent his last hours sitting on the wrong type of throne to pass to his son and the money had gone.

John had a first wife Avisa of Gloucester and a second wife Isabella of Angouleme. Queen Isabella was implicated in an attempt to kill King Louis of France but she had the sense not to attend the trial. She tried to stab herself and after this shut herself away from the world by taking the veil and keeping out of the limelight. She died in 1246.

HENRY III
1216 to 1272 (born 1206)

When his father, John, died in October it was only a matter of days before the celebrations stopped and Henry was crowned.

Crowned was not perhaps totally accurate as his mother leant a piece of gold bling for the job due to his father losing the crown jewels. Very young, just nine, Henry had help from others including William the Marshall and Justiciar Hubert de Burgh as well as Archbishop Langton. By 1232 Henry dismissed de Burgh and the other two had died so he was able to show all his own irresponsibility.

He was devoid of all the characteristics of good leadership and he upset all levels of society. Because of extravagance he allowed the church to be depleted of money and followed this by making sure the state was near bankrupt as well. How he managed such a long reign is incredible.

Although the handling of finances was as bad as his father managed he was actually very different in that he was a pious man. His God-fearing attitude was probably his salvation.

In 1258 he summoned parliament to get money to pay the pope, however Simon de Montfort opposed this and soon they were at loggerheads with de Montfort actually winning a battle at Lewes and taking charge. Eventually son Edward did reverse the fortunes by winning at Evesham.

Henry was losing mental ability from 1270 and certainly from 1271 he was suffering until he died peacefully, obviously senile, on 16th November 1272 after 56 years and 20 days, reign. He was buried at Westminster Abbey with his heart taken to the Abbess of Fontevraud as he had promised her, no doubt she was pleased.

His wife, Eleanor of Provence, became a nun and died in 1291.

Kings of England and Wales

EDWARD I, LONGSHANKS
1272 to 1307 (born 1239)

Henry's oldest child became the actual Edward the First, although there had been a few Edwards before him. He was considered a great king by his own folks, but not the best of friends with the neighbours. Probably efficient and living a blemish free private life he was not surprisingly thought of as a good bloke in England.

He was away on the sixth crusade when his father died, so he rushed home eighteen months later. First he set about the Welsh.

After beating the Welsh he did reform some laws and even arbitrated between two claimants to the Scottish throne. In 1294 he had an argument with the French and started to fight them. This led to the Scottish king Balliol joining the French which was a bit mean considering the help he had been given.

Off to Scotland went the English king. Balliol was replaced by William Wallace (Mr. Braveheart) and Edward won the battle at Falkirk quite convincingly. Trouble continued until 1305. Edward captured and hanged Wallace who was replaced by Robert Bruce as the adversary.

In 1304, at the siege of Stirling Castle the English king had a few near death escapes. Once a bolt from a crossbow glanced his armour and stuck in his saddle, this did not amuse him as he pulled it out and used some choice language to explain his discontent. Later a huge stone was thrown from the castle which could have squashed him, it missed, but given half a chance he would have thrown it back, so he immediately built a massive trebuchet to do just that.

As a result he won the siege.

The king died at Burgh by Sands (north of Carlisle) still fighting, although by then 67. He had been getting weaker and actually died while trying to be helped out of bed, just when he was preparing another attack on the Scots.

His great wish was for his son to carry on the fight and carry his bones until the Scottish were under control. Unfortunately his son had other ideas and buried him in Westminster Abbey, along with his wife Eleanor. On his tomb is the famous inscription "Edwardus primus Scotorum malleus hic est" or "here lies Edward I hammer of the Scots".

The death of Edward's first wife was a sad affair. He was in Scotland of course but when she died he had a cross erected at each nightly stopping point on the funeral procession's journey to London. The last one was famously at Charing Cross and she was buried in Westminster Abbey.

He also married Marguerite of France who outlived him by 10 years. She too had a monument erected in her memory by Edward II at Greyfriars Church, but years later a Mayor of London sold it with other royal tombs for 50 quid. Some mayors are not appreciative of statues and memorabilia.

Scotland

A bit about Scotland is worth noting in 1286, for example, King Alexander III died accidentally when his horse fell off a cliff with him on it, at Kinghorn in Fife.

He was followed by Margaret who was only 3 in 1286. She came from Norway and died in Orkney from severe sea-sickness in September 1290 which led to Edward choosing John Balliol to take over until deposed in 1296 and he died in 1313 aged 63.

Although William (Braveheart) Wallace was handed to Edward I and soon hanged, drawn and quartered, the lead in Scotland moved to Robert I (The Bruce) who died of natural causes in 1329. He beat Edward II at Bannockburn after learning to be patient from a spider. His son followed as David II.

EDWARD II

1307 to 1327 Deposed (born 1284)

Son of Edward I and a very different character, his death has to be the most horrible and the most painful possible. Historians have pointed to the fact that he was raised away from his parents to explain some of the differences in his character. Certainly his father's wish for him to continue the fight against the Scots was never understood and that concept was so important to his father that an independent observer might conclude that they never met. Daddy had provided him with a playmate, Piers Gaveston, when he was a boy and Edward was very pleased. He loved hunting and outdoor pursuits.

As a homosexual Edward got comfort and advice from Piers but this was not appreciated by all.

Edward put an end to the war with Scotland by losing the battle of Bannockburn decisively in 1314.

Gaveston was a brash character and he became particularly unpopular however the king's cousin, Thomas of Lancaster, stopped the relationship at Warwick when he met him at the roadside and chopped his head off.

These were vicious times and the king got revenge later. Also they were times of hardship and famine.

The king's wife, Isabella of France, was 13 when they married and it is an understatement to say they had little in common. It was not a good start when he gave some of her jewels to Piers and she had a great friendship with a person called Mortimer. As a result of this liaison they deposed the king and he fled only to end up imprisoned in Berkeley Castle in Gloucestershire. When there he was murdered by Gurney and Maltravers at the instruction of Lord Berkeley. Isabella is naturally a strong suspect for having involvement in the instruction to get rid of the king showing the importance of being pleasant to wives. The method of death was supposed to be symbolic, with a red hot poker shoved up his anus. This left his body in good enough condition to lie in state, and he was buried in Gloucester.

EDWARD III

1327 to 1377 (born 1312)

The son of Edward II took over as with his mother's help he had deposed his father. Mortimer was a great help to the pair of them until his authority became a problem and he was sent to Tyburn for dispatch. Edward III turned out to be chivalrous, efficient and a popular winner. His grandfather would have been proud of his efforts against the Scots. However his reign also involved the kingdom fighting the Black Death and the start of the Hundred Years War with France. Edward's son, known as the Black Prince, did particularly well taking on the French but then moved on to Spain where he got ill and the disease eventually killed him.

Edward became increasingly enfeebled and took to enjoying the company of low life. He had an insatiable lust which got out of control when his wife, Phillipa of Hainault died in 1369. He died at Sheen in 1377 when his body was robbed by prostitutes who had been companions*. So he died in disgusting circumstances in sharp contrast to his early competent life. A warrior reduced to a mess (although we will never know if he was happy). A stroke actually caused his end.

There was a theory that he was buried with his horse but he is actually buried in Westminster Abbey without it. Perhaps the horse objected.

*Some historians have been a bit cruel to the prostitute Alice Perrers who has been recorded as the person who stole the rings off the king's fingers while he was still warm. This was a bad move, but the king's wife was dead and some say Alice was originally a lady in waiting for the queen and then a good help to the king, who had a different idea of what she was waiting for.

"Now, what can I take for my pension fund?"

RICHARD II

1377 to 1399 deposed (and then died 1400)

There was a reason for Richard II being deposed and that was his nastiness and with it his incompetence. He was the son of the Black Prince (real name Edward of Woodstock) who had been the oldest son of Edward III. The Black Prince has been considered a model valiant knight and his son Richard was known as a tyrant who was unjust and extravagant. He put down the Peasants' Revolt led by Wat Tyler. Poverty and illness were rife in his time.

Richard's father, the Black Prince, was Edward III's eldest son, but his second son was John of Gaunt and it was his son who was Henry of Lancaster soon to be Henry IV. In 1399 Henry came out of exile and deposed King Richard and took control. Richard was locked up in Pontefract Castle in Yorkshire and he most likely starved to death there in 1400. The Wars of the Roses are often recorded as taking place from 1455 to 1485 but some of the seeds of conflict come from this reign.

❧ House of Lancaster ❧

HENRY IV

1399 to 1413 (born 15th April 1367)

In 1399 Henry of Lancaster (also known as Henry Bolingbroke after the castle of his birth) came out of exile in France to seize the crown (and his lands) back from the unpopular King Richard II. Not that any of his reign was easy as the Percy family were against him and he had problems in Wales from Owen Glendower. Parliament accepted him next.

He spoke English as his main language which was a rarity and much to his credit.

He was a well-travelled man aged 32 when he took charge and was said to be religious despite his treatment of Richard and also he did execute the Archbishop of York.

Henry IV had an illness for the last years of his reign which has been described as a skin affliction and it may well have been leprosy. There have been other suggestions including epilepsy with a skin problem and even heart disease but leprosy is the most recorded. The problem was it killed him on 20th March 1413. He was buried in Canterbury Cathedral.

HENRY V

1413 to 1422 (born 1387)

The eldest of Henry IV's four sons, another Henry was described as a dashing prince. He fought for his father and got his reputation as a great warrior. At the Battle of Shrewsbury he had an arrow removed from his head which involved cleaning and disinfecting with honey and alcohol.

When the throne was his he was straight into action setting about the French with a good deal of success. He laid siege to Harfleur and it collapsed and he won the Battle of Agincourt. He spent most of his reign fighting in France, returning to England with his bride Catherine of Valois for a short spell (her father was king and mental). He had left his brother Clarence behind in France, but because he was killed the king returned to France where he got ill. The illness soon got worse. His chamberlain thought it was pleurisy but other people thought it was dysentery. He was carried on to Bois de Vincennes where he died. The final cause of death was likely to be dysentery although heat stroke was also considered as it had been a scorching hot day of travel.

His victories have given this king a strong reputation as a great English leader with a son to take over, and continue, although that was a bit of a hope as he was only weeks old.

HENRY VI

1422 to 1461 (born 1421, Deposed and died 1471)

When his father died Henry VI was hardly ready to rule as he was under one year old. His uncle, the Duke of Bedford took charge of the French territories and another uncle the Duke of Gloucester took charge of England. The French business did not do so well particularly because of the rallying efforts of Joan of Arc. She was then tried and burnt at the stake in Rouen but nothing improved over there until a truce was agreed in 1444 and Henry married Margaret of Anjou.

From early in the reign there were problems from factions in England and these grew to become the Wars of the Roses. The Duke of York was a claimant to the throne as a descendant of Mortimer in line from Edward III and eventually parliament recognised him as Protector.

In 1453 the king had a peculiar problem in that he became incapably mental. The illness had a few dates put on its inception but 6th July at Clarendon in the New Forest seems to have been an important date for the problems to be considered outstanding. The king rallied to take part in a battle at Watford with the Duke of York and troops, where the king got an arrow in his neck.

The mental problems continued but his wife naturally did not want her husband to lose the crown because she had a son who would not inherit if the line moved to York.

At the battle of Wakefield the Old Duke of York did not have 10,000 men and the Lancaster forces were fully manned to siege Sandal Castle. When the duke was up he attacked the army down the hill and did well with his limited troops, but half way up the hill he was killed probably near where the Manygates memorial to him was placed. The queen had won a decisive battle and was hugely pleased. The king thought he was a tree at the time but the acting head of state was dead. However the grand old duke had sons and battles continued to the bloodiest fight ever on English soil at Towton where the Yorkists won.

The king was still mental, and he hid in the hilly country of the Pennines for months probably still thinking he was a tree, but no longer in charge. He was later caught in Clitheroe Wood and taken to the Tower of London for a five year stint. He did escape for a time in 1470 but this only led to a short exile for the Yorkist, Edward IV, and soon Edward was back to power and Henry was back in the Tower. Henry and supporters lost the Battle of Tewkesbury and all was lost for him. He died in the Tower, stabbed while praying the next day, although the press release was that he died of melancholy and displeasure (with a knife in his back).

His wife was the power behind the throne and she was captured at the Battle of Tewkesbury where her son was also killed and where Edward regained the throne for Yorkists. Margaret spent years in the Tower and was there while her husband was violently dispatched. Later she was ransomed and returned to France to live out her final years, dying in about 1482.

Henry had founded Eton and King's College, Cambridge and the provosts of these lay flowers annually on the altar which now stands where he died. Many people now recognise his effort to educate the poor and his hatred of war. Today he might be considered to have been woke, yesterday he was thought to have been weak, but at the time he was thought to be weird.

Scotland

In Scotland James I ruled from 1406 until 1437 when he was assassinated at Perth by Atholl (his uncle) and Robert Graham. He had been a sensible king, a poet and musician and had benefited from a time abroad. He had been in English hands for a while but was also ransomed in 1424 to return until his violent death. James I was replaced by James II in 1437 but the new king had only been born in 1430. He ruled until 1460 when he died while his men were trying to retake Roxburgh from the English. Unfortunately for him a cannon exploded next to him while being fired at the English.

JAMES II of Scotland

"Boom! Okay we need to move on to James III."

✤ House of York ✤

EDWARD IV
1461 to 1483 (born 1442)

Son of the Duke of York and victor of the Wars of the Roses, so far, was not a very nice man. He took over the country during King Henry's reign by winning the Battle of Towton in March 1461 and later after murdering him had complete control.

Edward had mistresses and illegitimate children but married Elizabeth Woodville (who had previously been married to a Lancastrian, Sir John Grey). He got good money from defeated Lancastrians, his mistresses, English tradesmen and the French all allowing him to live flamboyantly. His younger brother became Richard III. However another brother had a horrible death arranged by Edward. That brother was the famous Duke of Clarence who was accused of treason by Edward and was killed in the Tower of London by shoving him upside down in a butt of Malmsey wine. There was no truth in the old joke that he got out three times to go to the toilet, he just drowned.

Edward never lost a battle but the future King Henry VII was alive and living abroad.

Edward almost certainly died of natural causes described as a loss of strength in pursuit of pleasure (dirty bloke). In York on 6th April 1483 there were Masses said for his soul on his passing. He actually died on the 9th April.

His health actually went down hill rapidly with ague or malaria picked up in 1475 from France being a major theory. Catching a chill while fishing in the Thames was another. Poisoning was also a feasible cause but being annoyed about the Treaty of Arras was probably the most unlikely of the theories given at the time for his death.

He left two sons who also feature in the nasty death stories of this period and five daughters.

His wife Elizabeth eventually retired to a convent in Bermondsey and died a poor woman. Her sons were soon killed in the Tower of London but her daughter, another Elizabeth, became Queen after marrying and combining the Houses of York and Lancaster. Her will left no worldly goods but in it she beseeched her daughter to pray "God to bless her and all her children", which was nice.

Scotland

JAMES III reigned from 1460 to 1488 when he was murdered after battling rebellious lords at Stirling (the battle with a wonderful name of Sauchieburn). The spooky version of the story is that the king lost and escaped the battle only to meet a mysterious priest who stabbed him. He was a superstitious king who enjoyed music and the company of friends but was not considered great at making decisions or doing the governing job.

EDWARD V

1483 to 1483 (born 1470)

This was a very short reign indeed and it has been much written about. At thirteen it was also a short life. He was said to be a charming youngster with good potential. His father Edward IV had two sons with Elizabeth Woodville and when father died the elder brother inherited the job with his uncle acting in the leadership role and as guardian until Edward V was old enough to take charge. It is reported that Elizabeth was worried for the safety of her two young sons right from when her husband died. She was in Ludlow but she did send the kids to London as arranged for uncle Richard to be their protector. The question is: Did Uncle Richard kill the two boys in the Tower of London? The answer seems: Very likely - yes.

Richard of Gloucester is the obvious chief suspect and gained a lot from the deaths, he later became king. Suffocation while in their beds has been the considered method of murder with their bodies quickly disposed of. Some children's bones were dug up by workmen at the foot of some stairs in the White Tower in 1674. They were in a chest, and assuming they were not the bones of two other children who happened to have been walled up in the Tower, they could well be their remains, but dating in 1933 proved inconclusive of their ages. In 1674 Charles II arranged the burial of the bones in Westminster Abbey.

Edward V had therefore a reign, although never crowned, from 9th April to late June and he and his ten year old brother (another Richard) disappeared. These were murderous times, his great grandfather was beheaded, his grandfather died in battle, his uncle Edmund was killed following the same battle as his grandfather, his uncle George, Duke of Clarence, was murdered by drowning, Uncle Richard III was killed in battle, his brother was smothered and half brother also died in the Tower, although possibly he had a heart attack in prison.

RICHARD III

1483 to 1485 (born 1452)
(Includes the end of the Wars of the Roses)

Richard of Gloucester became king on the death of the two boys in the Tower.

He was obviously no saint and the best of his available defences is that he was unlikely to be a callous assassin, nastier than Hitler in the eyes of some historians, and prepared to take the risk of denying his poor young nephew the chance to rule. He may have poisoned his wife as well, but this again is supposition.

Richard soon after arriving in London started to make arrangements for his coronation and he put the two boys in the Tower. Buckingham helped but then had to be executed for insurrection. Sadly Richard's son died.

Richard actually can be remembered for some good legislation, and there is an alternative case in his defence. He had been loyal to his brother Edward IV and had held the family together. He was the protector of the youngsters and acting regent. He was also considered a moderate man and sensible, with fewer executions taking place in his term. He never announced the death of the children. If the children did not really die until 1485 when Henry VII was king there is a different slant on the whole affair and it is during this reign that the story is written. There has also been doubt about how much of a hunchback Richard was although deformity helped to label him as evil at that time.

As for the death of Richard III, that was very clear. In 1485 Henry Tudor landed back in Milford Haven and prepared troops from Wales and England. The ensuing battle took place at Bosworth Fields near Leicester and Richard was killed in battle. Perhaps he was wandering around looking for a horse and his crown ended up on a thorn bush. He was slaughtered, bringing an end to the Wars of the Roses. His body was treated unceremoniously and he was buried in Leicester, under a car park as has had much publicity. Found again in 2012 he has now been formally identified from the bones and put to rest in Leicester Cathedral, and it is now considered to be totally correct that he had a back deformity.

"I was doing better on White Surrey, why has she left me?"

❦ Tudors ❦

HENRY VII

1485 to 1509 (born 28th January 1457)

At the battle of Bosworth when Richard fell his crown was picked up by Lord Stanley and placed on the head of Henry VII. This ended the War of the Roses as Henry married Elizabeth of York (daughter of Elizabeth Woodville) and thereby combined the two factions, he represented Lancaster and she, York. The combined houses became Tudors.

Henry was a good politician and the finances of England were improving.

Henry was the grandson of Owen Tudor, (the second husband of Queen Catherine of Valois the wife of Henry V) hence the family name.

There were two rebellions in Henry's reign. The first involved Lambert Simnel who claimed to be the Earl of Warwick but Henry showed everyone the real Warwick to disprove that one and then Perkin Warbeck claimed to be the younger brother of Edward V, the child from the Tower of London killed by Richard III (or by Henry himself). Warbeck was executed anyway. Simnel also had a bad outcome, he ended up doing the royal washing up.

Although recognised as a good king as his kingdom was settled, money was tight for the population. He did help the wool industry and playing cards were established with pictures of his wife on them. He did not have known mistresses.

His wife died soon after giving birth to her seventh child on her 38th birthday in 1503.

From 1501 his health was said to be a problem, he may have started to go blind. Health problems continued until he died possibly of a stroke or much more likely he actually died of tuberculosis, at Richmond Palace in 1509 aged 52.

He is buried with his queen in Westminster Abbey.

HENRY VIII

1509 to 1547 (born 28th June 1491 died 28th January 1547)

When his father died on 21st April 1509 Henry took the throne but his daddy had actually once wanted him to be Archbishop of Canterbury. It turned out that he had a big influence on the Church of England.

The famous poetry that reminds us of this reign, and his many wives, is:

> *Divorced, Beheaded, Died,*
> *Divorced, Beheaded, Survived.*

But which one did which is a bit more difficult for children to remember.

Henry was a successful tyrant. His argument with the pope over the annulment of marriage number one (to Catherine of Aragon) gave him the opportunity to be supreme head of the church and he arranged for an English translation of the bible to be available in every church. He also dissolved the monasteries from 1535 taking their lands and possessions and actually sharing the spoils among noblemen as well. He used his share of the estates to develop the Navy (and to get rich).

He had an older brother Arthur who married Catherine of Aragon first but he died before his father in 1502 from a viral respiratory illness while in Ludlow Castle. The illness was called English sweating sickness, or flu.

Henry's first wife Catherine had problems producing an heir and this set the theme for Henry in life. He had problems producing a son and this became an obsessive problem.

Henry started his reign a fit bloke. Latterly he became obese as can be seen in the Holbein picture in the National Portrait Gallery. His leg started to be more and more painful which meant he often had to be carried about. It is little wonder he became irritable and his porters would also be little pleased. He died slowly in agony with first signs of the "sorre legge" in 1528 which was varicose ulcers or perhaps a bone infection, an accident in 1536 could also have added to the problem and Anne Boleyn thought this contributed to her miscarriage.

Many suggestions have been given for his ill health including malaria, gout, alcoholism, osteomyelitis, cardiac infection and a favourite, syphilis. Venereal disease was unlikely as there was no treatment of it noted in his records (but the others on the list could all or any be accurate). His condition deteriorated until he died in 1547 at Westminster after 38 years reign and six wives with just one son and heir. Off he went to the great banqueting suite in the sky, or perhaps he just became a banquet for a multitude of worms.

CATHERINE of ARAGON

Queen from June 1509 to May 1533
(born 1485, died 7th January 1536 Divorced)
(although Henry saw it as annulment)

Originally married to Arthur (who died), her father in law, Henry VII, also wanted to marry her, but then third to like her, Henry VIII, married her instead, although she had problems producing the heir. All her children died except the future Queen Mary. It was a theory for some that marrying his brother's ex-wife was bad luck and caused the problem, Henry even claimed the marriage was not legal for this reason when conversing with the pope. Henry actually had an illegitimate son by a lady in waiting, a Duke of Richmond. His divorce caused the row with the Catholic Church and the invention of the Church of England.

Catherine set about helping the poor and lived on until dying in January 1536 in Kimbolton Castle. There have always been conflicting opinions as to how much the king, or Anne Boleyn, mourned the death. Cancer is now considered to have killed her as a description of her heart seems to suggest this, and although at the time poisoning was rumoured it was most likely a natural death.

She is buried in Peterborough Cathedral.

ANNE BOLEYN

Queen from 1533 to 1536
(birth date lost in Norfolk. Beheaded)

The lady in waiting to Catherine was certainly doing just that, waiting for Henry, but only marriage would do. She was therefore instrumental in the evolution of the Church of England. She was born in Norfolk at Blickling and her sister was a mistress for Henry.

Henry and Anne formally married on 25th January 1533. Her task was to produce the future king but she did the next best thing by producing a future famous queen. Where Catherine had Mary, Anne had Elizabeth.

She was convicted of treason on 15th May 1536 and beheaded four days later. It was said that she went to her execution with dignity.

"I helped to start the Church of England and now look what's happened."

JANE SEYMOUR

Queen from 1536 to 1537
(died 1537 Birth date not known. Died)

Jane had been a maid of honour for Catherine of Aragon and the dispensation allowing Henry to marry her was issued on the day Anne was beheaded. Her intention was to serve the king and very soon she did. She quickly became pregnant and she managed to produce the vital son. The effort killed her. It is said she told the attendants to save the baby and put his life ahead of hers, and the king was making the same point. She died a few days after the birth at Hampton Court and her son was taken to Havering-atte-Bower for safe keeping until he ruled.

Jane haunts Hampton Court annually on the anniversary of her son's birthday and so does Katherine Howard but she pops up for people to see on a less organised basis. Anne Boleyn chooses 19th May to show herself at Blickling Hall, her birthplace, and also sometimes on her execution date, and she has been seen at the Tower of London as well at odd times, and at Windsor Castle etc. She still gets about England.

Jane is buried next to Henry at St. George's Chapel in Windsor and was the only wife to get a queen's burial ceremony.

ANNE of CLEEVES

Queen from 6th January to 9th July 1540
(died 1557 birth again not known. Divorced)

Wife number four, and Henry was getting a bit desperate. He asked the king of France to send three princesses but this was not agreed to. It took a couple of years for Anne of Cleeves to be chosen for him. When he met her he was not as keen as she had a more masculine appearance and a pitted face after smallpox and Henry described her as "like a great Flanders mare".

Henry had to marry her for diplomatic reasons but made it clear he was not happy. She did not speak English, but probably picked up the message. Henry arranged for a group of religious leaders to find a way out of his marriage and they concluded that he had been tricked into it. The marriage was declared unconsummated and annulled.

Anne was pensioned off with £4,000 per annum, estates and jewels and not sent to the Tower as expected. She was friendly and helpful to the three children who were future rulers and she died seventeen years after her spell as Queen, outliving the other wives. Even buried in Westminster Abbey, she has to be described as a bit lucky.

KATHERINE HOWARD

Queen from 1540 to 1542.
(born 1522. Beheaded)

Katherine had a rather boring and neglected youth but she had some "flirtatious unions" (or good times) including with her cousin Culpepper, but then the king took notice. She was described as a bit on the plain side of good looking and when Anne of Cleeves was removed she was soon married. Very quickly though there were rumours about her relationship with Culpepper who was a member of the king's privy chamber, and an old suitor called Francis Dereham returned from Ireland to be her secretary. After time, when the king got the news of the rumours they were all three arrested. When she was taken from Sion House to the Tower of London it was by barge and as she entered through Traitors Gate she could see the heads of her suitors on spikes to welcome her in. The night before her execution she had a practice at putting her head on the block and this upset her maids and she died proclaiming her love for Thomas Culpepper.

KATHERINE PARR

Queen from 1542 to 1547
(born 1512, died 1548) Survived
(Henry died 1547)

The final wife had already been married to Lord Borough when very young and he died when she was still a teenager. Then she married Lord Latimer and he died. Her third marriage was to the king who was 20 years older than she was (and he died). They got on well together but Henry's leg was getting worse and so was his temper. The big bust up had to come one day and as expected it did. The story was that Henry made legal arrangements for her to be arrested but that the document was picked up by her maid in a corridor. Katherine realised the danger and had hysterics declaring herself ill. Henry heard she was ill and in remorse had himself carried to her bedside. They kissed and made up.

A few months later Henry's light went out and she was able to marry an old suitor called Seymour (her fourth marriage). She retired to Chelsea with £1,000 cash and £3,000 in jewels but was soon pregnant and unfortunately although she gave birth to a girl she died a week later of complications from the birth.

EDWARD VI
1547 to 1553
(born 1537)

Henry did have one son with Jane Seymour (wife number three) and he was Edward VI and although just ten he was already a precocious brat.

He was able to speak seven languages and actually enjoyed listening to theological arguments. Unfortunately he was also a bit weak and never very healthy. His advisers included a couple of dukes, Somerset and Northumberland.

Northumberland's son, Lord Guilford Dudley, had been married to Lady Jane Grey who was the granddaughter of Mary the sister of Henry VIII. While ill the young king named her as successor. Tuberculosis was the most likely cause of his ill health, but he probably also suffered smallpox and measles in his time although in the end it is said that he caught a chill at tennis and developed a cough. Some who said he was poisoned were sent to the pillory. He died, not yet sixteen at Greenwich.

No chance of him having a son but the title did not immediately go to a half-sister.

LADY JANE GREY

1554 to 1554
(born 1537)

Jana Regina, or Jane Grey, was Queen for nine days and hers was a sad story in brutal times. She was sweet sixteen and the granddaughter of Mary Tudor who was sister to Henry VIII. Not a very substantial claim to the throne and this opinion was particularly held by Mary who was the eldest legitimate child of Henry VIII.

Lady Jane quickly married Guilford Dudley before young Edward died. Her claim was that both Mary and Elizabeth were children of marriages that were annulled by their father. Public opinion was more in favour of Mary (Jane was Protestant and Mary was Catholic).

Jane was arrested and sent to the Tower of London. From her room she could watch the scaffold being erected. Her husband was dispatched first and she could see his coffin taken past her window on its way to St. Peters Church nearby. On a misty February morning she was next. Nine days a queen and then dumped under the stones of St. Peter ad Vincula at the Tower.

Lady Jane Grey haunts her family home as many queens of that time do. She can be seen in Leicestershire on the anniversary of her execution, 12th February.

"There goes my husband."

MARY I, BLOODY MARY
1553 to 1558

Daughter of Henry VIII and Catherine of Aragon, Mary was a staunch Catholic despite her father. Her nickname Bloody Mary was accurate as she executed the Archbishop of Canterbury, Cranmer, and bishops Latimer and Ridley and many more. Protestants were at big risk. Never a happy monarch she spent her youth away from her mother. When she married King Philip of Spain she failed to have a child. She was a bit of a misery and so he left her. Although she wanted him back he did not return.

During her reign England lost Calais, our last outpost on the continent.

Cancer overcame her and she died in 1558 after a short time in charge. She had a lot of problems in the baby making body areas, including amenorrhoea (without menstruation). These problems also caused years of headaches and heart palpitations. Mental stress no doubt added to her problems and general demeanour. She very likely died suffering cancer of the womb and there was a flu outbreak at the time as well.

After she died in November 1558 at St. James' Palace she was buried in the same tomb as Elizabeth I later used in Westminster Abbey, without a monument.

ELIZABETH I
1558 to March 1603
(born 1533)

Elizabeth was Protestant, and known as the Virgin Queen. Difficult times had existed throughout her early years. She managed to avoid political and most importantly, religious debate (it is said she usually went to bed). Known to be vain, independent and unscrupulous she was also short of money. This was the time of Shakespeare, and also Drake and Raleigh who made England respected or sometimes feared. It was also the time of building priest holes and deciding who to shove in them and when. Catholics had to be very careful.

The next chapter deals with the problem Elizabeth had with her neighbour Mary Queen of Scots. Elizabeth ruled England to her end and during her term the Spanish Armada was defeated and the Catholic advances rebuffed. In 1570 the Pope excommunicated her and this made the intrusion of Catholic Scottish Mary a problem in England.

It is said that she reluctantly agreed to the execution of Mary.

Elizabeth's death was a bit weird as she insisted on sitting upright for three days fully dressed and obviously about to peg out, an old lady. She sat in the audience chamber at Richmond Palace refusing remedies and food and not speaking. She had a throat infection which had made swallowing impossible, then pneumonia set in and she became semi-conscious, eyes open until she died. Her courtiers seem to have been in touch with Scotland. One story was that Robert Carey, who later became Earl of Monmouth, got notice of the death. He then rode off to Scotland to inform James and three hours after getting the news James was in England.

She was said to have a bleached white and marked face with contrasting ugly teeth. Her looks were not good for a picture at the end of a successful reign for England.

Scotland

MARY Queen of Scots

Queen of Scotland 1542 – 1567
(born 1542 died 1587. Beheaded)

Mary was Queen from just six days old (the only surviving child of her father James V who died of fever, although some said he died of grief after losing the battle of Solway Moss, but fever seems likely). She was raised in France with the intention of her being the wife of the dauphin Francis, who became King. That made this Mary Queen Consort in France and Queen in Scotland but also a great granddaughter of Henry VII of England. She was a devout Catholic and this caused her a problem in Scotland and England.

Her French husband died when she was 18 and this tragedy was followed by a couple of disastrous marriages. First to Lord Darnley, and she may have helped murder him. Then she married Bothwell who was even more of a suspect in the case of the blowing up of Lord Darnley.

Mary suffered porphyria which has been a problem in the royal bloodline (literally as it is a blood production problem and can be a very upsetting illness).

The increase in Protestantism in Scotland led to Mary having to get out of the country and into England where Elizabeth was initially tolerant. However the presence of Mary was a threat to Elizabeth as she was supported by Spain. The Babington Conspiracy caused Elizabeth to fear for her future and therefore Mary had to be controlled and she was imprisoned or restricted in a large number of venues, Workington Hall, Carlisle Castle, Bolton Castle, Tutbury Castle, Wingfield Manor, Ashby de la Zouch Castle, even Chatsworth and also Sheffield Manor, Buxton, Chartley, Tixall Hall and of course Fotheringhay Castle. She had a good tour of England but Fotheringhay was the last place she stayed. By this visit she knew her fate and on 8th February 1587 she lost her head. She mounted the block with dignity and it took three blows to remove it. There was a gap of six months before her burial.

As Elizabeth had no child the Tudor clan had fizzled out and because Mary had a son the royal line merged with Scotland.

James I or VI had Fotheringhay Castle raised to the ground and his mother buried in Westminster Abbey.

❈ Stuarts ❈

JAMES I (or James VI of Scotland)
1603 to 1625
(born 1566)

A very different character from his mother he was the great-great grandson of Henry VII. Great-great was the way he saw himself but others were not as convinced. With little charm he was a clumsy chap with a tongue too big for his mouth. Bad table manners and a lot of drooling meant he was not the best guest at dinner parties. Court life was extravagant and he was probably homosexual, yet he married Anne of Denmark and evidently campaigned against sodomy.

It was this king whom Guy Fawkes wanted to blow up. James actually believed strongly in the divine right of kings. However he was also tolerant of Catholics which along with his efforts to unify Great Britain and his commission of the bible that carries his name meant he was known as "the wisest fool in Christendom".

Arthritis took a grip on him in later years and he most likely also suffered porphyria like his poor mother (called the tertian ague or now perhaps tartan ague). After a hunting expedition at Theobalds in March 1625 he fell ill and three days later may have had a stroke, and he became speechless. He may also have had dysentery but the porphyria symptoms could have been the problem. It is worth noting that he died leaving the country broke.

Despite the finances his funeral was lavish.

CHARLES I
1625 to 1649
(born 1600)

Charles was a weak child but became a strongly opinionated adult. He believed in many of his father's ideas and most importantly the divine right of kings (God intended him to rule). When, prematurely, he got to meet his maker this may have given him some advantage over others but little advantage on earth.

These were the days of "Puritan revolution" when many believed in purifying or simplifying church services. Politically the rights of people were being thought about. Charles was finding opposition on both religious and political grounds. Civil war was the result and one side had to win.

Charles came to the throne in a financial mess. He was described as handsome, courageous, and very moral but also broke. The king had to raise money and introduce taxes without parliamentary authorisation. After months of wrangle in 1629 the king dispensed with the need for parliament and went it alone for eleven years.

The Civil War started in 1642. Cromwell led the parliamentary forces, also known as "Roundheads" (or New Model Army) and Charles was at the head of the "Cavaliers" or Royalists. Both sides were fairly equally successful for the opening years.

In June 1645 the king took a crushing defeat at Naseby in Northamptonshire. He fled to Scotland but into the hands of "Covenanters" who imprisoned him and handed him to the Parliamentarians.

Poor Charles tried hard to get free, arguing his cause vociferously. Some of his incarceration was more like house arrest so he tried a couple of escape attempts. When on the Isle of Wight it was difficult to go far.

To the end he believed he should govern the country. His trial was a bit of a farce. Described as a traitor, a tyrant, a murderer, and as public enemy number one he was found guilty. His death was unique and partly due to his own obstinacy and his own political and religious beliefs (poor Lady Jane Grey might dispute that statement).

The execution took place on 30th January 1649 outside the Banqueting House in Whitehall. About two in the afternoon he lost his head in a single blow. He was buried in St. Georges Chapel Windsor as Westminster Abbey was out of bounds for him.

Charles also had a distinguished wife, Henrietta Maria, daughter of the King of France (they wanted a boy but she came instead). Her father was assassinated within hours of his coronation. She was betrothed to Charles at fifteen and spent a difficult life between France, Holland and England. When she came to England during the Civil War she landed in Bridlington (but not for a holiday). The Parliamentarians bombarded the town and Henrietta spent the night in a ditch. She embedded herself in the heart of her husband's army and with him when reunited at Oxford. She avoided capture and retreated to France again and was in the Louvre when she heard of her husband's execution. For days she could not speak.

Years later she was cheered by the news of the restoration of the monarchy and the knowledge that her son was King, but very soon after that her youngest son died of smallpox. Bad news was never far from her.

In August 1669 she had trouble sleeping and was given a potion by her doctor to help. Soon after her heart stopped and her life of love, ups and downs was over.

"The divine right of kings may help him where he is going."

The Commonwealth – 1649 to 1660

OLIVER CROMWELL (Lord Protector)

1649 to 1658
(born 1599)

The king lay headless and England had no king. The next period was soon a military dictatorship under Oliver. He did not take well to reasoned debate but had been a great general. So he became Lord Protector, a post very similar to King. He took on the Dutch and the Spanish but his home policy was the Puritan struggle.

He is known as humourless, sombre, strict and overall gloomy, but actually he smoked and drank, hunted and played bowls, loved horses and music and probably had vices as well. His public image remained devoid of fun.

Dictatorships work well until the man dies. On 3rd September 1658 this happened. The Honourable Member for Huntingdon died of malaria in Whitehall and his son inherited the title of Lord Protector. The funeral was similar to any provided for a king and clearly better than that given to Charles. Crowns were seen and he lay in state at Somerset House (although it was an effigy lying in state not the corpse).

For kings their fortunes after death can be both up and down and this is also true for Lord Protectors. After the restoration Charles II dug Cromwell up and had his body dragged through the streets of Tyburn, hanged, beheaded and finally to make sure no further problem could come from him his head was stuck on a spike. It remained on view for about seventeen years until a gale blew it down. A soldier picked it up and gave it to his daughter, who may have been pleased as she sold it and eventually it found its way to Cromwell's old college, Sidney Sussex College, Cambridge. So after a chequered career his head came back to his old home of knowledge. It was buried by them last century in a secret place in the college grounds so that students do not dig it up again.

RICHARD CROMWELL (Lord Protector)

1658 to 1659
(born 1626, died 1712 after 20 years in exile)

When his father, the big chief, died, the idea of hereditary succession sprang to mind and Oliver's third son became the Lord Protector. A quiet and private man he obviously had none of the fire of his father and the job of Lord Protecting was not ideal for him. It was not long before General Monk set off to meet Charles II and Richard Cromwell resigned. In 1660 the monarchy was restored. By the time the true king was welcomed back Richard had skipped abroad.

He lived in Paris for a long time under the name John Clarke and even kept this name when he did return to a quieter life in England in 1680. When he died at Cheshunt on 12th July 1712 he did not get the lavish funeral of his father. He was simply buried at Hursley in Hampshire.

The Restoration

CHARLES II
1660 to 1685
(born 1630)

The Merry Monarch (an easy epithet to take on after Oliver Cromwell's idea of party Britain).

How Charles II escaped the parliamentarian army is a story worthy of a good comic full of "daring-do". After the battle of Worcester he fled, keeping his head down, via Wolverhampton to Lyme Regis and Charmouth, calling at Cirencester en route. He headed inland to Salisbury and as all good tourists should, he visited Stonehenge. Famously he hid in an oak tree and disguised himself as a servant to avoid detection all in his six week dash to get to France. With a ransom of £1,000 on his head it is amazing that about 40 people did not betray him.

The escape was achieved and exile became his way of life. But every dog has his day and when Cromwell died the spaniel (or son of spaniel) got his call for a return.

He was a selfish man with morals that were far from perfect. A courtier said of him "he never said a foolish thing nor ever did a wise one". He had wit and probably charm. He also had spells of depression but he was quite popular and this was helped by him riding a few winners at Newmarket.

By the time of his death he had a number of children but unfortunately none with his wife, Catherine of Braganza.

Sadly this reign was marked by the Great Plague which killed 70,000 (still a big number) and the Great Fire of London (which destroyed 13,200 homes and upset the great diarist Samuel Pepys).

Success against the Dutch, and in America (including naming New York after his brother) along with stable government gave Charles a good reputation. Also he died of natural causes.

He had a night of drinking with the Duchess of Portsmouth, one Sunday but the next day had a stroke or apoplectic fit. This happened on 2nd February and he died on 6th February 1685 with the famous dying words "I have been an unconscionable time dying, but I hope you will excuse it". Polite to the last, he made the comment because he had many visitors while ill. As expected some people suspected poisoning and he certainly had a cocktail of medicines from doctors trying to help that may have done damage. He may well have had a series of strokes or in the end kidney failure (possibly Bright's disease). During his final days he also swapped privately to Catholicism. His actual final words were reported as "Let not poor Nelly starve" because he cared for Nell Gwynn as she had entertained him well.

JAMES II

1685 to 1688
(born 1633 died 1701. Deposed 1688)

Brother to Charles II and son of Charles I he also had a life in exile. He was a good soldier, and he organised the Navy. But he was not well liked by many, including his own family. Once again religion played a part in his popularity and ability.

He was Catholic and favoured Catholics in important jobs. A Protestant relative, the Duke of Monmouth, organised a rebellion in his reign. More importantly he had a daughter who was a staunch Protestant and she married William of Orange (a reference to his Dutch origins and not his colour).

Parliament did a bit of negotiating with daughter Mary and her husband and in 1688 they arrived in England and James left at speed. He lived in France and soon gathered troops and went to Ireland. In 1690 he lost an important battle, the Battle of the Boyne, with son in law taking the honours for the Protestant cause.

So a religiously muddled era of British life led to James back in France at the Palace of St. Germain for the rest of his life. His daughter ruled but he spent a large proportion of his life in exile. His father had been beheaded with religion a dominant factor in his downfall, causing early exile. His brother had ruled as a Protestant, but died a Catholic. He was defeated as a Catholic and his daughter took over his throne as a convinced Protestant.

A confusing state of affairs, added to by a confusing state after death.

In March 1701 he had an attack of partial paralysis and taking the Bourbon Waters did not cure it. Unlike so many people for whom a drop of Bourbon and water would have revitalised them James worsened and after a couple of weeks, he died. James wished for his body to be buried in the local parish church of St. Germain en Laye but this was not to be. Bits of him were distributed all over. His bowels were buried as he wished locally, his head with brains were sent to the Scots College in Paris and it is not clear how pleased they were. His embalmed body went to the English Benedictine monks in Paris.

He failed to be canonised as he would have wanted but a few happenings were attributed to him after death. So once again he nearly made immortality, but failed. His body hung around and during the French revolution the coffin was broken up to collect the lead. It was George IV who arranged a burial for him in 1824 a long awaited full burial for at least the big bits.

Some royalty have difficulty breeding but James had eight children by his first marriage and only seven by his second wife and quite a few illegitimate ones as well. Only three legitimate ones survived him. Queen Anne was the most important but Louisa Maria Theresa died in 1712 and the third he called James III (but those in power called him something else, often rude but also "The Old Pretender").

❋ Orange ❋

The famous reign of WILLIAM and MARY

Just to summarise: Charles I (Catholic), then Cromwell (Puritan Protestant), Charles II (Protestant except last days), James II (Catholic), Mary and William (Protestant).

Religion was very influential.

WILLIAM III

1689 to 1702, and MARY II 1689 to 1694
(Mary born 1662 William born 1650)

The married pair consisted of James' daughter Mary, and William III, whose mother was the daughter of Charles I (another Mary).

They ruled together but while William was away Mary took charge, otherwise William was the boss.

Mary was plump when young but grew tall, and was light hearted and a bit of a care free extrovert when young but she grew more serious. Never very healthy but in 1694 she had smallpox and on Christmas Day it was announced that she was going to die. She was at Kensington Palace with a drove of doctors who did plenty of bleedings and fed her cocktails of potions. She improved a bit but the doctors probably were not helping a lot and she died on 28th December 1694 aged 32. Outside the door was a priest who sat for the final days and then on her death he dashed off to see her father James who was in exile. It was a long journey to carry the word and the priest got quite ill on the journey so the message missed the mark and William carried on alone. Her greatest memorial has to be the Serpentine in Hyde Park and that is loved by many.

William of Nassau, Prince of Orange, was said to be a bit stunted, but this is not obvious from many pictures that exist today. He was asthmatic, and he could be quite formal and reserved in company, and also he could have been homosexual. Outwardly they were a very devoted couple that had ruled together, but now he was on his own. He had a desire to crush the French which was particularly strong when the French recognised James' surviving son as James III.

In 1701 William's legs started to swell. On 20th February 1702 he was out riding his horse Sorrel when it stumbled on a molehill. William fell and broke his collar bone. The accident happened near Hampton Court where he went to recover, but his arm swelled and he caught a chill which became fever and on 8th March 1702 he died.

This is why his Jacobite enemies (supporters of James, the Old Pretender) would raise a glass and make a toast "to the little gentleman in the black velvet waistcoat". Never was a mole so popular.

❈ Stuart ❈

ANNE
1702 to 1714
(born 1665)

Queen Anne succeeded William in 1702, she was his sister in law. At times she was a bit more friendly towards her father James II (in exile) than her sister Mary ever was, and also at times friendly to her half-brother James who was known in France as James III, and in Britain as the "Old Pretender". This situation was at least partially why she carried on after William with unfriendliness towards France.

She had two close friends, Mrs. Masham and Sarah Churchill whose husband was to lead the troops and was made Duke of Marlborough.

These two friends helped so that Anne's reign is remembered as a good one. Wins at Blenheim, Ramillies, Oudenarde, and Malplaquet and our control over Gibraltar are all from this time. The queen was described as dull, nasty, greedy, sly, unproductive, crass, spoilt, idle and good at cards. Despite this she was considered unattractive to men. The Act of Union with Scotland was made at this time. She was the last sovereign to preside over Cabinet and the last to practise the "King's Evil" which entailed touching people with illness or deformity to help cure them. She touched Dr. Johnson in 1712 but it did nothing for him.

Anne gave birth to a number of kids but only one lived any real time and he was the Duke of Gloucester who lived to his eleventh birthday. He had the condition called water on the brain and was a weak child. That birthday night he was taken ill and he soon died. This left Anne the last Stuart and without an heir. Her husband was Prince George of Denmark who was generally not noticed and he died of dropsy on 28th October 1708. (Dropsy sounds peculiar and it is, edema, or now often called water retention). Any history books that mention Queen Anne having excellent legs are sadly referring to the style of furniture named after her. She had to be carried to the Abbey for her coronation in pain from gout.

Anne died on Sunday 1st August 1714 after a few months of poor health, she put on a lot of weight. Her coffin was said to be almost square. The death was thought to be from stroke with the addition of pain from gout and she had abscesses and fever. The actual cause is still not clear with syphilis ruled out and the family porphyria also unlikely although she probably had an obvious fever at the end which could have been from bacteria or a virus.

A Jacobite Bishop set off to get the said James III but this was not going to happen as parliament wanted a Protestant. It was another wasted journey.

After Anne's death the succession went to the nearest Protestant relative of the Stuart line. This was Sophia, daughter of Elizabeth of Bohemia, James I's only daughter, but she died a few weeks before Anne and so the throne succeeded to her son George.

❋ The Hanoverians ❋

GEORGE I
1714 to 1727
(born 1660)

Great grandson of James I, George was next to be in charge although there was a theory that he was not too bothered. He took a few weeks to arrive, (and some wished he had not), he seemed disinterested, was thought of as cold and calculating, and it seemed he did not want to take an active role in politics. A major reason for this was that he did not speak English.

He did not get on too well with his wife, she was already locked up. However there was a good side to this situation. The king found he could sell important positions and titles and parliament could take decisions without his input. Robert Walpole became Prime Minister and the power of the realm, but sadly in this reign the South Sea Bubble burst and ruined many finances.

George spent his last years squabbling with his son.

One night in June 1727 he was returning to his favourite home and on the road near Osnabruck when he suffered a paralytic seizure, or as we would now say a stroke, and dropped dead. It was claimed that a rough crossing on his rushed journey to his beloved home had caused the illness.

Although he was dead he did visit his mistress, the Duchess of Kendal, or so it was said. He turned up at her apartments in Hampton Court but after death he was a big black crow. The conversation may have improved (the crow may have used English) but the visits were probably upsetting for her.

George probably never loved his wife Sophia Dorothia of Celle and the clue to this was that he locked her away for 32 years. Before he was King they had children including George II. He kept her quiet but she protested innocence over her earlier friendship with a count called Königsmarck and when she died in 1726 she was unable to be buried at

Ahlden as George had required, due to flooding. She was taken at dead of night in an unmarked coffin to Celle.

There was a story that she had written a letter to argue her innocence to her husband and describe her feelings which had helped a little to ease her time imprisoned. It stated that at the Pearly Gates he would need to explain. The story continues that in the dead of night on that June date in 1727 the letter was thrown into the carriage carrying the King and that at the end of the journey the king was found dead.

"We thought that crossing was rough, we can't be too surprised."

GEORGE II
1727 to 1760
(born 1683)

Because son George was opposed to his father his popularity on taking the throne was high. He was similar to his father in that he was money grabbing, selfish, and also spoke little English, but there was a big difference in that he had a wife who lived with him and could influence him positively. He could be quick tempered and therefore the relationship between him, his wife and Walpole (the Prime Minister) was important to bring success.

Then came the wonderfully named War of Jenkins' Ear, and disastrous relations with Spain and the resignation of Walpole. This gave the king the power to take sides in the Austrian War of Succession. George II became the last King of Britain to lead his troops into battle at Dettingen in 1743. Against an army twice the size of his, he won.

He was never a great father and had little time for his eldest son Frederick who died in 1751. Poor Fred one day experienced a great deal of pain, and a lot of coughing as he threw himself back, dead. This has been put down to a blow from a tennis ball years earlier, and better still a blow from a cricket ball (he loved cricket) but actually he probably had lung disease. Death by cricket would probably be his preferred choice having gone.

A London paper gave a famous epitaph to Prince Frederick:

> *Here lies Fred,*
> *Who was alive and is dead,*
> *Had it been his father,*
> *I had much rather,*
> *Had it been his brother,*
> *Still better than another.*

Had it been his sister,
No one would have missed her,
Had it been the whole generation,
Still better for the Nation,
But since 'tis only Fred,
Who was alive and is dead,
There's no more to be said.

(Anon - Quoted by William Makepeace Thackery in The English Humourists The Four Georges The Oxford Dictionary of Quotations cites Horace Walpole, Memoirs of George II vol I, p436).

The poem came from a Jacobite and the last threat from that side of the family was extinguished in this reign. No longer a threat from the man called James III (in France) or the Old Pretender, but this time from the Young Pretender, the son Bonnie Prince Charlie. Like his father he landed in Scotland and drove his way south as far as Derby. He lost the Battle of Culloden with King George having a resounding win, thanks to the Duke of Cumberland ("Butcher" Cumberland as he was known). Poor Bonnie fled to France with the help of Flora MacDonald, and died addicted and pickled by alcohol in Rome.

As for the great leader of the troops, George, in stark contrast to his gallant days he died by falling off the lavatory. At 7.30 in the morning on 26th October 1760 at Kensington Palace a valet heard a loud noise of wind (as we say) and a groan and on entering the toilet he found the king with a gash on his right temple. The King tried to speak but died. The actual cause of this famous incident may well have been a heart attack.

GEORGE III

1760 to 1820 (born 1738)
Also known as Farmer George

He was the grandson of George II, and Frederick was his father, George was not only born in England he was also English speaking, the first to be able to claim that since Queen Anne. He took a genuine interest in the British Kingdom. During his time America was lost and this is why he was considered careless and obstinate. He insisted on collecting taxes from that colony and that upset them. Other colonies and possessions were held by hard work and good military successes during his reign.

Farmer George was different from other recent kings in one big way. He went totally bonkers. Like Mary Queen of Scots he had the family illness porphyria, which today is treatable. For example, he got the idea that all marriages had been dissolved, but lots of hen-pecked husbands found this was completely bogus. He stopped his carriage in Windsor Park in order to have a long conversation with the King of Prussia, who looked very much like an oak tree to everyone else who saw the event. The conversation went well. His condition worsened and he lost his sight as well as his mental capacity. He clung to his family and particularly needed his wife (she died a bit before him which he did not understand) and he died from his condition on 29th January 1820 the longest serving monarch so far, at nearly 60 years.

Spookily some guards reported seeing him in his sparse rooms after his death. They saluted and continued their rounds.

Never a very popular king, George had been intelligent and his decline was certainly sad. A leader of fashion and an improver of royal residences it is a pity that he is remembered for wearing a straight-jacket.

His wife Charlotte was influential and no doubt patronised great music including Handel and she was the great influence behind the importance of Kew and the gardens. She died peacefully at the age of 74 in 1818, and was considered by many to be the first British queen to have distant black antecedents.

GEORGE IV
1820 to 1830
(born 1762)

In true continuance of the Hanoverian line up to this time, this king was not well liked. Some polls have rated him next to King John in the unlikeable stakes. He had an extravagant lifestyle and he treated his queen badly (Queen Caroline of Brunswick). She got support from the public during her legal battle with him over whether she had an illegitimate child.

He spent money like water (a constant flow), and he drank cherry brandy like water as well. It was as if the revenue system was set up to provide him with pocket money and hospitality.

Although overweight he was a stylish dresser and able to attract women. He had a dozen or so lovers as well as a few one night stands. Yet he was known to be rude and crude. History has given this king a bad press and yet there are very nasty characters who have in some way managed to be more popular. This king was very pro Britain and the Navy, he loved Brighton and its pavilion, and he was very supportive of Protestantism.

For a considerable part of his reign George suffered from arteriosclerosis which could have killed him at any moment. From April to June in 1830 he struggled with dropsy (or water retention) which caused his limbs to swell and kept him in pain. One day he is said to have commented to Robert Peel that he would be dead by the weekend and true to his word on 25th June he coughed and groaned in his chair and dropped dead. He died in his cottage at Windsor with his mistress Lady Conyngham, after an excess of cherry brandy.

His heart was found to be swollen in his huge body but the cause of death was described as a haemorrhage in his stomach and that was attributed to his coughing.

WILLIAM IV

1830 to 1837
(born 1765)

The third son of George III was already in his 65th year and not a fit man when he became King. He was a warm character and there were stories of him wandering up and down St. James's Street talking to strangers and shaking hands. He had a stable family life after an early liaison with an actress, Dorothy Jordan. The Reform Act of 1832 was significant in his reign. He was known sometimes as the sailor king, and he had known Lord Nelson in his youth. William had one very impressive achievement and that was the large number of pubs that were named after him. Monarchs were having a hard time in the world but William was liked, happy and unconcerned.

He suffered asthma badly and also his age created a problem that indicated to all that it was not going to be a lengthy reign. He had fits of fainting with the breathing difficulty and his heart was weakened. He did keep going until May 1837 when he died at Windsor with his final cryptic words being "The church, the church"?

So he was buried in St. George's Chapel which is very like a church.

VICTORIA
1837 to 1901
(born 1819)

It was expected that Victoria would take over from Uncle Bill. Her father was the Duke of Kent and he was younger brother of William IV and therefore she was granddaughter of George III. At 13 she had done a tour of Britain to study problems of poverty and at 18 she was Queen. She was considered to be lively, she loved dancing, music and food. Three years after starting her reign she married Prince Albert of Saxe-Coburg and Gotha.

Queen Victoria continued to increase the respect for royalty that William had managed after the Georges. She faded from public attention for a section of her long reign but Britain was changing and developing, and with her husband she was involved in committees to improve life where possible.

They worked well together and were in love. He was her private secretary and then Prince Consort.

Albert suffered serious stomach cramps in August 1859 and although he recovered he had a chronic problem. He suffered leg pain and back pain for his last weeks. On 9th December 1861 his doctor concluded that he had typhoid and he died at 10.50 p.m. on 14th December 1861. The ongoing problems from his stomach pain and his final illness may have been due to Crohn's Disease, kidney failure, or possibly stomach cancer.

The queen was obviously devastated and remained in mourning (to her end, she never gave up on matters of state but she spent most of her time in Windsor Castle or at Osborne, her home on the Isle of Wight, with visits to Balmoral). Her nickname "the Widow of Windsor" was accurate although she would have said she was not amused.

Just under 100 million people were her subjects at the start and by the end of her turn it was 240 million under her rule.

Her end came in 1901 with support from the Kaiser. She retired to Osborne (but still dealing with matters of state) with eye problems, rheumatism and aphasia (the loss of mind associated with old age). Her last word was "Bertie" a reference to her eldest son (she had nine children with Albert). What she was about to tell him we will never know.

She drifted in to a coma in the end and at 6.30pm 22nd January 1901, she died. She was 81.

At 64 years, that was the longest reign at that time for a British monarch but she was only three days older than George III had been when he went to his maker.

When the queen knew she was leaving this world she considered it important to ensure she was well endowed for the next. She dictated pages of instructions for the funeral and gave a list of items to be included in her coffin. This list included jewels, necklaces, bracelets, and rings (one of which had belonged to the mother of John Brown). For extra clothing there was her husband's dressing gown and his cloak (made by dead daughter Alice) and her wedding veil. She included photos and a plaster cast of Albert's hand to hold on to when required. There was also Balmoral heather for added memories.

It seems she may have believed in the afterlife.

"Any sandwiches?"

❋ House of Saxe-Coburg and Gotha ❋

EDWARD VII
1901 to 1910
(born 1841)

His mother's last word "Bertie" may well have been intended to be a sentence telling him to be more like his father, or be more serious in outlook. She need not have worried because at 60 he had no practical administration experience but he took to the responsibilities of the job immediately. He negotiated with foreign powers, and British politicians, with skill. The Boer War found a negotiated conclusion, and he improved relations with France. He had a sobering influence on the Kaiser who was building his Navy and he obviously did not want wars.

There was genuine sorrow when he died. He was not totally fit at the start of his term; he had chest problems. He liked Biarritz for winter holidays and in 1910 he stopped in Paris in March for the theatre on his way back to Blighty. He caught a cold and undid any help the French coast had given. It did improve but when at Sandringham he deteriorated and had real problems getting his breath. He returned to London but the illness continued to be disastrous and then his horse won at Kempton. Not that the win helped very much but his last words expressed pleasure at that happening. The queen realised he was on the way out and called for his mistress to come to him, Alice Keppel. His heartbeat weakened and at 11.45 p.m. on 6th May 1910 it stopped and Halley's Comet reached its peak in the night sky.

More than 350 thousand people filed past his coffin as he lay in state. The famous story of his funeral procession was that it was led by his faithful terrier Caesar who followed his dead master (on a lead attached to a Scottish soldier).

❋ House of Windsor ❋

GEORGE V

1910 to 1936
(born 1865)

When his father died there was a constitutional crisis in full force. The Irish were promised home rule by the Liberals and the House of Lords were blocking legislation. Added to this there were strikes, the Suffragette Movement and not long until the worst war ever. George II may have been the last to lead troops into battle but George V had to visit troops in trenches who were losing comrades in appalling conditions in the First World War.

The Irish problem continued and after the Great War got worse along with more strikes until they developed into the General Strike in 1926.

Extreme problems but the king made broadcasts as technology developed with a voice that sounded helpful, reassuring and sincere. His image was one of dignity and reliability with an old style.

Several years before his death septicaemia had affected his heart. When he visited Sandringham at Christmas 1935 aged 70, he caught a cold. His heart was weak and he could not get his strength back, and he had breathing difficulties. He died at 11.55 p.m. on 20th January 1936. He was buried at Windsor.

Recently there have been allegations that his doctor, Lord Dawson, (then President of the Royal College of Physicians), may have given the king a "euthanasia" injection of morphia and cocaine so that he did not suffer a lingering end. It is claimed that Queen Mary and the Prince of Wales asked that if his condition was terminal he should not be allowed to linger. There was also a theory that it was thought better to have the news in morning papers rather than evening ones. Some would add him to the list of those monarchs murdered, but he was certainly fading fast.

His final words are also a bit disputed. The famous phrase was "bugger Bognor" a reference to the conversation with the medic who was giving hope by suggesting that the king could soon recuperate in his favourite seaside town, Bognor Regis. Unfortunately the King did not feel up to it. The physician who actually gave the medication reported his final words as "God damn you".

EDWARD VIII

June 1936 to December 1936
(born 1894) Abdicated

When Edward flew to London in 1936 after the death of his father he was popular. He had been educated at Oxford and had served in the army in the war in France. He had travelled the world but also interested himself in home affairs. But by the time of the death of his father the American press had already noted his interest in Mrs. Simpson from their land. During the Autumn of 1936 the rumour of marriage between them was growing. Marrying commoners was not the problem, Henry VIII and Edward IV had both done that. Mrs. Wallis Simpson had divorced, and twice. Eleanor of Aquitaine had a first husband still alive when she married Henry II. In this case the choice became stark, abdication or abandon his loved one. Just before Christmas 1936 he abdicated and they became the Duke and Duchess of Windsor. The marriage stood the test of time and the Duke died in 1972 just before his 78th birthday. Queen Elizabeth visited him at his home in Paris while on a state visit just over a week before his death. He already had advanced cancer of the throat by then.

He had a fitting burial for a king and was laid to rest at Frogmore.

His wife died in Paris in 1986 after suffering dementia for her final years.

GEORGE VI
1936 to 1952
(born 1895)

Edward's brother George was said to be shy and he had a bad stutter, but he also evidently had some of his father's important characteristics, steady and sensible qualities. He had served in the Navy including at the Battle of Jutland in the Great War. When King he had the problem of dealing with Hitler in Germany. He stayed in London when the war started in 1939 and bombing soon began. He gave comforting broadcasts and lived through the thick of the troubles including Buckingham Palace taking a bomb itself.

After the war Britain had to recover and his reign saw that difficult regrowth taking place. He was never in strong health. In 1948 he recovered from a thrombosis in his right leg without it having to be amputated. In 1949 he had a right lumbar sympathectomy to help his back. By the end of 1951 he had influenza and found it difficult to get over it. It was found that he had a patch on his lung and his surgeon Sir Clement Price Thomas had to operate to remove the cancer. The king had his left lung removed in an operation in the dining room at Buckingham Palace. Recovery was going to be slow.

On 31st January 1952 his older daughter, Elizabeth set off on a royal tour of Australasia in place of him. The king went to the airport to say goodbye for what was the last time, and then he returned to Sandringham but within a week he was dead.

At the start of 6th February about midnight a policeman had seen the king adjust a window catch in his bedroom but in the morning of that day he was found dead. Elizabeth was told while she was staying at Treetops in Kenya, on her way to Australasia.

There is now no doubt that his death was smoking related.

Final information

The stories in this book have all added to the folklore of the United Kingdom. Many may even be true, all are well known. John of Worcester stretches the imagination a bit with his belief that a dead saint killed Sweyn. Other stories have a very credible ring to them. The Grand Old Duke of York has been given a variety of dates for his life and he may not have been the bloke killed in Wakefield after all, (some say it was Fred, son of George II) but perhaps the nursery rhyme may not have given a truly accurate record of events.

The job of ruling in Britain has never been an easy one, in fact it has been downright dangerous as most would perhaps expect to find in this book, many reaching violent ends. Killed in battle may have been expected in turbulent times as happened for Harold, William the Conqueror, Richard Coeur de Lion, Edward I and of course poor Richard III. Being executed perhaps not as easily foreseen for Charles I but several Queens before him had that fate. Anne Boleyn very famously ended her life in that style followed by Katherine Howard then later Jane Grey and Mary, Queen of Scotland. But after Charles I getting his head removed it is interesting that Cromwell too was executed, only in his case over two years after he had died of natural causes, which will not have worried him too much. This was also the outcome for Harold I and he will not have noticed. Smoking has been blamed for the last few deaths considered and illhealth while being obese for several others including famously Henry VIII, Queen Anne and George IV.

Sadly one day there will be an opportunity to add to these chapters and let us hope it is in many years time. Let us also hope that there are many more chapters to follow the next. These pages have described the deaths of a very diverse group of people who have all influenced the nation they served. They had pedigrees that included Anglo Saxon, Celtic, Scandinavian, Norman (French), Dutch, German, but also many other countries and regions through marriage. The future looks wonderfully varied and prosperous and the recipe has produced a vibrant multicultural nation that is capable of a rosy future.